"Norma Swanson, herself, is the epitome of a Christian lady with 'class' . . . [Her] book meets a major need in the Christian community."

> Paul A. Kienel
> *Executive Director, Association of Christian Schools International*

"Young people will love this book! Old ones, too, for that matter."

> Ruth Bell Graham
> *Montreat, North Carolina*

"Owning *Dear Teenager* will be like having a friendly and awe-inspiring encyclopedia at one's fingertips. *Dear Teenager* is *must* reading for every teenager, parent, and teacher."

> Genevieve S. Klein
> *Regent Emerita, The New York State Board of Regents*

"Clearly picture[s] a lifestyle informed by the Holy Scriptures . . . [and] provide[s] detailed guidelines for Christian responses to almost all situations teens face today."

> Victor A. Constien
> *Executive Director, Board for Parish Services, the Lutheran Church—Missouri Synod*

"Just as Nancy Reagan advises just say 'no' to drugs, Norma's good advice is to be selective and gracious in one's relationships by saying 'please' and 'thank you.'"

> The Honorable Helen Marie Taylor
> *The United States Representative to the United Nations*

"[With] this book, Christian teenagers will learn how to behave as Ambassadors of the King of Kings."

> Jack Wyrtzen
> *Director, Word of Life Ministries*

"Mrs. Swanson writes in the tone of a knowledgeable aunt who has the teenager's best interest at heart. . . . *Dear Teenager* is an excellent way for Christian young people to learn the 'how' and (more importantly) the 'why' of proper manners in contemporary America."

> Dr. John Holmes
> *Association of Christian Schools International*

"There is a wonderful emphasis on attitude, kindness, consideration, unselfishness, graciousness, responsibility, and thoughtfulness. Surely these are the traits we pray for in the lives of our Christian young people."

> Jean Martz
> *Walnut Creek (California) Christian Academy*

"One of the great blessings that comes from spiritual revival is the reformation of manners or the restoration of courtesy to society. . . . *Dear Teenager* provides both colorful descriptions of proper social etiquette and also the biblical rationale behind it."

> D. James Kennedy, Ph.D.
> *Senior Minister, Coral Ridge Presbyterian Church*

"In a permissive society permeated by mediocrity and decreasing standards, *Dear Teenager* reinforces the need for, as well as the rewards reaped, when excellence and discipline are practiced."

> Linda J. Cunningham
> *Former Director, The Katharine Gibbs Business School, Vienna, Virginia*

DEAR
TEENAGER

DEAR TEENAGER

Norma Swanson

OLIVER
NELSON

A Division of Thomas Nelson Publishers

NASHVILLE

Published in Nashville, Tennessee, by Oliver-Nelson Books, a division of Thomas Nelson, Inc., Publishers, and distributed in Canada by Lawson Falle, Ltd., Cambridge, Ontario.

Unless otherwise noted, the Bible verses used in this publication are from THE NEW KING JAMES VERSION. Copyright © 1979, 1980, 1982, Thomas Nelson, Inc., Publishers.

The Scripture quotation noted NIV is taken from the HOLY BIBLE: NEW INTER-NATIONAL VERSION. Copyright © 1973, 1978, 1984 by the International Bible Society. Used by permission of Zondervan Bible Publishers.

The Scripture quotation noted KJV is from The King James Version of the Holy Bible.

Appendix C, Principles of Music Evaluation, is excerpted and adapted from Word of Life's "Rock Music" from the *Teen Student Manual*. Used by permission of Word of Life Fellowship, Inc.

Printed in the United States of America.

ISBN 0-8407-9558-0

Contents

Foreword

This book is long overdue. It is a book that gets to the basics of daily courtesies as well as reinforces admirable qualities of character. The author does a remarkable job of reintroducing the amenities that once were commonplace among young people.

Norma Swanson is a vivacious Christian educator, full of creative ideas that spring forth in this book. Her key thoughts on character traits are essential to the full development of young men and women. Readers cannot help feeling that Norma is right on target and that her book will positively shape students now and in the days ahead.

A dedicated Christian, the author is a friend to teachers and has a wealth of experience to share.

Art Nazigian
President, Mid-Atlantic Christian Schools
Association; Past Chairman, Board of Directors,
Association of Christian Schools International

Acknowledgments

During the many months I worked preparing this book, I was continually uplifted by family and faithful friends who share my concern for a return to traditional values and the niceties of life that are so apt to be bypassed in our society.

I wish to express my sincere thanks to the following people:

George, my husband, for encouragement to begin the writing project;

Dr. Arthur Nazigian, who originated the idea;

Nancy Swanson, my dear friend who typed and retyped the manuscript;

Dr. Paul Keinal for his enthusiasm and expression of need for such a book;

Bill Bowman for literary assistance;

June Jones, my sister, and *Connie Brown,* my sister-in-law, who kept me informed of teenage attitudes toward fashion;

Lois Ferm for her support and encouragement;

Lila Empson of Oliver-Nelson for her patience and advice as she guided me through the process from pen to page.

My prayer is that the message of *Dear Teenager* will sink deeply into the hearts of young people everywhere, that they may grow in the likeness of Christ and that they may express through their interaction with others the love and respect so aptly taught us by the Master in His Word.

DEAR
TEENAGER

The Real You

*P*lease and *thank you* were probably among the first words you were taught to say. After you learned to recognize your family members and call them by name, your next word was probably *please*. It may have sounded more like *pwese* or *peas,* but it represented your parents' conscious attempt to teach you good manners. The simple word *please* shows consideration to another person. It turns desires into requests rather than demands. Somehow, "Please, may I have a cookie?" carries more respect and influence than "I want a cookie."

Do you have an etiquette?

Much of today's formal etiquette originated in the French royal court during the 1600s and 1700s. The nobles drew up a list of proper social behavior and called it *etiquette*. This word came from an old French word meaning "ticket."

Etiquette today is followed by all classes of people, and it is modified as social changes occur. Still, however, it provides a form of behavior to help us act in ways that make life easier and more pleasant.

Good manners are established rules of social conduct. They are desirable because they give us self-confidence and help establish pleasant relationships with others. They are based on solid principles given to us by God in His Word, the Bible. Good manners are to human behavior what traffic rules are to safety. Without them, life would be chaotic, and it would be unbearable to live with one another.

"Love does no harm to a neighbor; therefore love is the fulfillment of the law" (Romans 13:10). *"Though I speak with the tongues of men and of angels, but have not love, I have become as sounding brass or a clanging cymbal"* (1 Corinthians 13:1).

It's especially important for Christian young people wanting to show "Christlikeness" to be aware of and practice proper social behavior. Everyone has manners, good or bad. They reflect the real you. They are good if they reflect respect and consideration for others and bad if they reflect rudeness, thoughtlessness, or immaturity. Good manners are basically good sense. However, some young people tend to become so involved in current fads (such as music, dress, and speech) that they spend little or no time thinking about how to behave properly. Some say, "Oh, I know how to act right when I *need* to." But that isn't knowing how to act correctly; that is only knowing *about* acting correctly. Only as you practice good manners and they become natural to you can it be said that you *know* good manners.

Good manners are basically good sense.

The worldly trend for young people has been toward an overemphasis on self-will and its echo, "I want my rights!" You must take a serious look at this attitude and see where you stand in relation to it. Ask God to show you. You may be surprised at how much this worldly philosophy has become a part of your life. Christ emphasized the opposite of wanting self-rights. He said, *"Whoever exalts himself will be humbled, and he who humbles himself will be exalted"* (Matthew 23:12).

Clean Hands, Clean Words, Clean Thoughts

O God, our Father, give me clean hands, clean words, clean thoughts;
Help me to stand for the hard right against the easy wrong;
Save me from habits that harm;
Teach me to work as hard, and play as fair in Thy sight alone as if all the world saw;
Forgive me when I am unkind; and help me to forgive others who are unkind to me;
Keep me ready to help others at some cost to myself;
Send me some chances to do a little good every day, and to grow more like Christ. Amen.

—William DeWitt Hyde

Good manners reflect your sincerity, your concern for others, and your respect for their rights. A little verse you probably remember from childhood, called the "golden rule," went like this: "Do unto others as you would have others do unto you." It was sometimes called a golden glove, and you pretended to put on gloves as you said each word. If you have forgotten your golden gloves, look now among your possessions and wear them proudly. Your life will be changed for a greater good than you can imagine.

"Therefore, whatever you want men to do to you, do also to them, for this is the Law and the Prophets" (Matthew 7:12).

When Adam and Eve, through disobedience, broke their relationship with God, bad behavior entered the world. Had that not occurred, this book would not be necessary. We would all behave well and in the likeness of the One from whom we were created. However, with the sin of Adam and Eve came bad behavior, very bad behavior. Through anger, one of their sons killed his only brother. Other grievous acts were committed against God and other people.

"The heart is deceitful above all things, and desperately wicked; who can know it?" (Jeremiah 17:9).

God looked upon His creation, and His grief moved Him to establish basic rules by which human beings were to live. You may know them—the Ten Commandments. But people still chose to disobey. Therefore, God sent His Son, Jesus, into the world to provide redemption for us through His death on the cross and His resurrection.

Jesus walked in poise and confidence. He was the very essence of good manners, showing compassion, respect, and consideration for others, even in the smallest details of life. He realized that good manners and mature behavior would be difficult for us. He knew that we, too, would be tempted. Therefore, He assured us of help along the way.

When the rich young ruler pulled Christ aside to ask what he must do to be saved, Christ saw evil in his life but did not rebuke him. He spoke to him firmly but gently. The Scripture says He loved him. When the chief priests and scribes tried to tempt Him by challenging His authority, He was direct but patient. Even as He hung from a cross His attitude was, *"Father, forgive them, for they do not know what they do"* (Luke 23:34).

Maturity means taking on more and more responsibility and doing what you know needs to be done without being told to do it. Your social growth must keep pace with your intellectual growth. Everyone has observed the sad situation of a person who has achieved intellectual status but has remained at the kindergarten level of social behavior.

"If anyone is in Christ, he is a new creation; old things have passed away; behold, all things have become new" (2 Corinthians 5:17).

As you walk through the pages of this book, take time to consider your own growth, your weaknesses or failures, and where you stand in relationship to the world. You will become aware of your increasing social responsibility so that it will become evident to others that you truly are of royal descent as you exhibit the kingly principles given to you in the King's own Handbook.

You—a winner every time!

Being yourself isn't always easy. Some young people just don't like themselves, and they cover up by attempting to project another image. They pattern their behavior and dress after someone they admire—too often someone who has gained recognition from the secular world. This is not "natural" behavior for them, and it is usually obvious to others that they are not being true to themselves.

"Do not enter the path of the wicked, and do not walk in the way of evil. Avoid it, do not travel on it; turn away from it and pass on" (Proverbs 4:14–15).

Each person is given unique talents and abilities. Yet

some people live their entire lives never realizing what valuable contributions they could have made to the world or how special they really are. How tragic to be a "could have been"! This does not have to be, however. As a young person, Roger Torrey Peterson, the famous artist for the Audubon Society, was unruly and directionless until a teacher helped him discover a talent that has brought joy into many lives. Helen Keller, blind and deaf from an early childhood illness, became an inspiration to the world as she overcame almost insurmountable difficulties. George Washington Carver, a poor Negro, endured discrimination and abuse as a lad to become a creative scientist who found multiple uses for the lowly peanut plant. A list of such persons would be inexhaustible.

Feelings of inferiority and self-doubt peak in adolescence. Most young people go through stages of feeling ugly or different. Physical appearance takes on a new importance as they strive to overcome those horrible feelings caused by imagining they are unattractive. These feelings are normal. You aren't the only one who has struggled with these pangs of "nothingness." Ask God to help you look inside to see what you really are and what talents and abilities you have; you can then develop them to add extra dimensions to your life and the lives of others.

Your personal identity is made up of many factors. You are a composite of your attitudes, manners, disposition, likes, dislikes and, of course, appearance. Many young women spend so much time on appearance that they woefully neglect other important areas of their lives, sometimes actually causing rejection by their classmates. Strive for a balance in all areas of your identity. The total of these areas accounts for "personality," and your personality determines how likable you are.

"But put on the Lord Jesus Christ, and make no provision for the flesh, to fulfill its lusts" (Romans 13:14). *"So then each of us shall give account of himself to God"* (Romans 14:12).

The desire to be liked, or to gain approval, is basic in everyone. Unfortunately, some young people sacrifice their own principles of character for the approval of their classmates. This is very dangerous behavior, often leading to a lifetime of regret. Your principles, as a Christian, may run counter to today's accepted behavior, and you may often feel like a fish swimming upstream. However, it is in this area of your life that your "Christlikeness" becomes most obvious and gives credibility to your faith. People who are a part of the secular world may not agree with you on your standards for a Christian life, but they will respect you and admire the courage you have to hold to your standards when opposition surrounds you. This evidence of character strength will open doors to reach others for Christ as they see something in you they would like to have. They will be curious and may ask you about it. Take advantage of the opportunity! Don't let them down!

As you mature, you will take on more and more responsibility. With responsibility comes decision making. You won't always be able to rely on friends and family. Often you will have to stand alone. It's reassuring to know you have God's guidance, but God does require that you bring *all* your attributes to Him. He works with the whole person.

Perhaps an illustration will make this clearer. You may have seen an old-fashioned rolltop desk with lots of little cubbyholes. Your life's experiences can be tucked away in your mind somewhat like you can tuck things away in the cubbyholes of that desk. As a situation arises for God and you to work out, He draws from all the "learned lessons" you have tucked away to help you with the new decision. He uses these lessons for guidance and direction. Listening and learning are essential to your future success.

"In all your ways acknowledge Him, and He shall direct your paths" (Proverbs 3:6).

You may feel anxious about the adult world you are entering. There will be many "firsts" for you, such as a driver's license, a bank account, and a job. Be assured that all young people have similar feelings. That is part of growing up. If self-consciousness plagues you, you may be comforted to know that it affects all young people. Self-consciousness is really just a fear of not being accepted. You can overcome it as you get the focus off yourself and onto others.

It's important that you learn what is expected of you and the rules of correct social behavior for specific situations. However, to provide a list of every situation you will encounter in life, with a corresponding rule for correct behavior, would be impossible. When you know the rules for specific situations, you will have developed the confidence needed to handle virtually every situation with poise. Remember, character is what you are when you are sure no one is looking. Add courtesy and a smile, and you will be a winner every time!

As you continue reading this book, it may appear that the price for Christian character and behavior is just too steep for a young person in this modern world. Should such thoughts come to you, please take a moment, dear young person, and consider the price Christ paid for *you*. Are you not willing to make any personal sacrifice for Him? Think about it!

"I will instruct you and teach you in the way you should go; I will guide you with My eye" (Psalm 32:8).

Chapter 1

Challenges

1. What are some ways in which you see young people attempting to model their lives after someone else? What dangers or benefits do you see in this?

2. How can you know what talents and abilities you have?

3. What area of "personal identity" do you consider most neglected by young men and women? Consider appearance, personality, Christian commitment, and so on. Explain.

4. What are ways in which young men and women can gain strength to face a secular society whose views on behavior do not agree with their own?

5. What are some of the benefits of knowing and practicing good manners?

6. On a scale of one (poor) to ten (excellent), rank yourself on your ability to resist ungodly influence from peers, television, music, movies, and so on.

7. Make a list of what you consider shortcomings or faults in your own life, with a corresponding list of ways to correct or overcome them. What positive results can you see for your life as you correct these shortcomings?

2

Your Proving Ground —Home and Family

Your home is your very special place of belonging. It's your family center, and good manners and correct behavior begin there. It's the *proving ground* where you can test your manners with those who care and understand. If you succeed at home, you will certainly succeed away from home. Your parents may insist on drill and practice. If that is the case, you are privileged. Your home provides an opportunity for you to learn social skills for successful relationships—now and future.

Harmony

A home may consist of one person or several persons. God established the family structure, placing the father in authority. In a home without a father, the responsibility of authority falls upon the next person in line, who is usually the mother. Children are subordinates under this authority. As God planned the structure, He also outlined the responsibilities of authority (father, mother) and subordination (children). God ordained this plan; human beings did not devise it. In His plan, love and respect prevail.

"For the husband is head of the wife, as also Christ is head of the church; and He is the Savior of the body" (Ephesians 5:23).

Unfortunately, not all homes observe God's chain of command and His character-building principles. The world system has stripped God of His authority, and in so doing, it has stripped the parents in the home of their authority as well. Many books and articles have been written on current philosophies, such as humanism, where all authority rests solely on the individual. Contrary to God's plan, the thinking of some modern philosophers leads only to chaos, despair, and destruction of the home and society.

Try as we may to resist the intrusion of these philosophies into our lives, they will creep in and raise their ugly heads. It is for this reason that Christian schools have been established—*to reinforce the concept of a sovereign God who cares for His creation and provides loving authority with guidance.*

If both of your parents do not observe or agree on God's authority, do not despair—all is not lost. You can personally accept God's authority in your life, and He will provide all that is needed for your growth and development. Many great men and women have come from such homes. As they depended on Him, they gained strength and wisdom. Some were even persecuted for their faith. But by their consistent respect for parents and by Christian behavior in the home, many families grew into a oneness and harmony with God and one another.

"The Lord is my light and my salvation; whom shall I fear? The Lord is the strength of my life; of whom shall I be afraid?" (Psalm 27:1).

Your parents play a vital role in your development. They are commanded by God to provide guidance *and* reproof. Good family relationships aren't automatic. They require cultivation and nurture just as any living thing. The term *generation gap* was popular a few years ago as experts tried to explain problems between parents and children. Such a *gap* does not exist in a home where God's chain of command is recognized and His authority is accepted and obeyed with

Home is where
   you can be heard
      without speaking a word,
   you are loved
      in spite of your flaws,
   your joy is shared
      and your sorrow divided.

love and trust. Parents aren't always without error, and they will admit to that. However, Christian parents have every right to expect divine guidance. Isn't it comforting to know that God is directing them as they, in turn, direct you?

"And these words which I command you today shall be in your heart. You shall teach them [God's laws] *diligently to your children, and shall talk of them when you sit in your house, when you walk by the way, when you lie down, and when you rise up"* (Deuteronomy 6:6–7).

God placed certain responsibilities on parents, and He gave responsibilities to the children as well: *"Children, obey your parents in the Lord, for this is right. 'Honor your father and mother,' which is the first commandment with promise: 'that it may be well with you and you may live long on the earth'"* (Ephesians 6:1–3). Obedience is a command, as is the honoring of your father and mother. God didn't say, "Until you are eighteen or until you can drive a car or until you get a job." Nor did He say, "Obey them only if they are Christians." God has given a special role to parents, Christians or not. Children are to obey; God will take care of the circumstances.

Some young people have ignored these commands and have insisted on "doing their own thing." Many parents are at a loss as to how to handle the difficult situations created when young people do whatever they want to do, regardless of parental concern and advice. And young people end up caught "betwixt two" in an attempt to please and be accepted by both parents and peers. A conflict arises that they can't resolve.

It's impossible to live up to the standards set by a home that observes God's principles and at the same time live by the standards set by a worldly culture. You have to make a choice. As the gap widens, the decision becomes more difficult. If you don't make a conscious decision, the evil forces of our day will take over and make the decision for you. You can be sure it will not be for God and righteousness. The drug culture that plagues us is, in part, a result of this gap between traditional values and current trends. When the pressure gets too great and a young person succumbs, the end result is disaster. (See Appendix E: "Betsy.")

Christians of all ages, but especially young people, are bombarded by temptations. As a result, some try to live as close to the worldly culture as possible without violating Christian standards. Entrepreneurs have built a multimillion-dollar business by taking advantage of this dilemma. Some Christians feel that the popular "rock" scene can be diluted and made acceptable by writing lyrics containing Scripture or phrases familiar to Christians. It is my opinion that this doesn't make such music acceptable to God. In dress and hair styles, in slangy language, even in fast food and colas, the world is trying to control your choices, to make you "one of them," to encourage you to be dishonoring to God. Young Christian, beware of the traps that have been set for you. Be sensitive and discerning. It's your life! (See Appendix C: "Principles of Music Evaluation.")

"But the Lord is faithful, who will establish you and guard you from the evil one" (2 Thessalonians 3:3).

Getting along

When conflicts arise (and they do), either with parents or with another family member, try not to participate. At an appropriate time, politely excuse yourself and find a quiet place where you can be alone to sort out your thinking. Consider all the factors involved, and then give them to God, one by one. This is a positive approach that works. It builds character while it disciplines.

"And be kind to one another, tenderhearted, forgiving one another, even as God in Christ forgave you" (Ephesians 4:32).

Arguing is self-defeating and causes hurt and destruction. Often people say harsh words during an argument that cause a lifetime of regret. A display of temper, at any age, is immature. It never resolves a conflict. A hurricane may last only a few minutes, but the damage it causes will be extensive.

"He who is slow to anger is better than the mighty, and he who rules his spirit than he who takes a city" (Proverbs 16:32). *"So then, my beloved brethren, let every man be swift to hear, slow to speak, slow to wrath"* (James 1:19). *"A soft answer turns away wrath"* (Proverbs 15:1).

Be sensitive and discerning. It's your life!

Many parents try to provide opportunities for their children that they were never able to enjoy. Wayward, undisciplined children who have been overindulged usually can't appreciate what has been given to them, and they cry out for more. In frustration, parents may try to provide still more. This indulgence leads to increased and more complicated problems. Wise young men and women consider the financial resources of their parents and are alert to what they can and can't afford. If you make a Christmas list of wants, make a corresponding list of what you can give. Love desires to give, not to receive.

Most parents make sacrifices to provide benefits for their children. They do this by choice. The fact that you are in a Christian school, or are being taught at home by Christian parents, or are encouraged to attend church or Sunday school or perhaps a summer camp, is evidence of their concern and sacrifice. Show your appreciation for your parents by being obedient and caring. Don't set unreasonable standards of perfection for them. Parents are people, too. Be generous with words of praise and gratitude, and you'll be rich indeed! (See Appendix E: "Jim.")

"In everything give thanks; for this is the will of God in Christ Jesus for you" (1 Thessalonians 5:18).

Ideas for creating and maintaining harmony within the family

1. Begin each day with a visit with God. However brief, it assures strength and wisdom. Prayer is a handclasp with God. (See Appendix A: "How to Have a Quiet Time.")
2. Respect the privacy of others by knocking on closed doors before entering rooms.
3. Take care of your room. Keep it neat; hang up your clothes or fold them and place them in a drawer.
4. Assume the responsibility of some household chores without being asked to do so.
5. Do your part in keeping household expenses down by careful use of electricity, hot water, and so on. If your parents approve, try to earn money with part-time jobs to pay for some of the "extras" you enjoy.
6. Be considerate in your choice of clothing by looking at the price tag *first*.
7. Respect schedules and routines of all family members.
8. Put the kitchen back in order after you eat a snack, or if it was not in order prior to your snack, assume the responsibility of putting it in order.
9. Respect the property of other family members. Don't borrow without permission.
10. If you borrow money, pay it back promptly.
11. If you must borrow an item and permission is granted, return the item as soon as possible.
12. Don't open or read mail not addressed to you.
13. Don't open a purse, a diary, a notebook, or anything of a personal nature.
14. Greet friends of family members with a cordial "Hello." Think of something kind to say to help them feel welcome in your home.
15. Contribute to the home and family atmosphere by being cheerful and pleasant. Keep your voice down, as well as any electronic equipment, radio, or television.

16. Help meet the needs of younger children in the family with your assistance and attention.
17. If grandparents are part of the household, include them in discussions and share your interests with them. Grandparents are great for encouragement. Show respect toward them. (See Appendix B: "Senior Adults—Grandparents.")
18. Be fair about telephone usage.
19. Be generous with "please," "thank you," and "may I?"
20. Be quick to apologize when you have spoken harshly or out of turn.
21. Keep family business within the home. Don't discuss it with outsiders. It is a good policy not to discuss private family matters with persons outside the home. If a serious problem arises and you feel you need counsel, go to your minister or a mature person who has proven to be a family friend.

Chapter 2

Challenges

1. Your home and circumstances may not perfectly fit the plan God has outlined in His Word. What changes need to be made? How can the changes begin with you?

2. Write a note to yourself outlining some positive steps you can take right now to make those changes. Put the note in a private place (to be reviewed later) and begin. God will help you. After a few weeks, check your note and compare.

3. Make a list of the responsibilities of a young person in the home as you feel God sees them. Provide appropriate Scripture to support your views.

4. How can you resist current godless philosophies and thoughts that take away the sovereignty of God and the authority of parents? Explain.

5. What can you do to resolve a conflict with family members?

6. List some of the traps or temptations that cause conflict between young people and parents, brothers, or sisters. How can they be avoided?

7. List ways in which young people can show appreciation and respect to their parents.

8. How important is your attitude in maintaining harmony in the home? Explain.

9. What acts of individual behavior have you observed that created havoc, hurt, or inconvenience to others? (For instance, parking in a no-parking zone.)

At Home—Your Special Place

Be it ever so humble, there's no place like home."
These words are from a popular song many years ago, but the
sentiment expressed is just as real and meaningful today. Remember the feeling of coming home from a great vacation
and stretching out on your very own bed? Pure ecstasy! Your
home gives you a very special feeling of belonging, and that's
how it ought to be. Be alert to an attitude of taking it for
granted that can creep in, envelop you, and cloud that sense
of gratitude. A good home doesn't just happen. It takes teamwork and the cooperative efforts of all who live there.

Neatness

A clean and neatly kept home reflects order and discipline, and it is enjoyed by everyone who enters. It is a compliment to the family members. Order is one of God's first laws.
This is evidenced in the story of creation. God had an orderly
plan for coordination and harmony, and He did it all in just
seven days! Order begets efficiency.
"Let all things be done decently and in order"
(1 Corinthians 14:40).
Most people are not naturally neat. Neatness must be
achieved. It's not that difficult to keep a home in respectable
"company" condition and still maintain a wholesome lived-

in look. However, it takes work, teamwork, and sharing, which are important elements in the building of Christian character. God has no use for laziness.

"Because of laziness the building decays, and through idleness of hands the house leaks" (Ecclesiastes 10:18).

The furnishings of your home were purchased with pride and perhaps some sacrifice. Some pieces may be antique, with sentimental value. Aunt Martha's silver compote dish may not mean much to you now, but as you mature, you'll gain an appreciation of its value and nostalgia. You'll better understand your parents' interests in such pieces. For now, accept the fact that many objects in your home hold special value for your parents, and treat them with respect. (See Appendix E: " 'Old Ivory.' ")

Good furniture can last a lifetime. It's unwise to assume that when it's worn out it will be replaced. You can maintain the furniture by treating it with care; for example, don't put your feet on furniture, lean back in chairs, or set a glass containing an iced drink on a wooden table without placing a coaster beneath it.

Clutter, which plagues every lived-in home, creates an atmosphere of confusion and disarray. You can help by picking up misplaced objects and putting them where they belong. This may mean Dad's newspaper or the shoes your brother kicked off while watching TV last night. If you left your popcorn dish by the sofa, take it back to the kitchen.

Being helpful in these ways will mean more to your parents than any gift you could give them. The special effort you make to keep your home a pleasant place for all who live there will show your maturity and your capability of enjoying the privileges of young adulthood.

Tabletime

Good manners are on display at the dining table, whether it is at home, a nice restaurant, the school cafeteria,

Our character is
but the stamp on our souls
of the free choices
of good and evil
we have made through life.

—Geike

or a diner. The same basic principles apply. (NOTE: Table manners are covered in detail in chapter 8.)

At home, go to the table promptly when you are called for mealtime, with your hair combed and your hands washed. Sit erect and be reverent, with head bowed and hands in your lap, while "Grace" is said. The custom of "Thanks" or "Grace" began with Christ. Throughout Scripture, Jesus took a moment to recognize and thank the Father for His gift of food.

"And Jesus took the loaves, and when He had given thanks He distributed them to the disciples, and the disciples to those sitting down; and likewise of the fish, as much as they wanted" (John 6:11).

Mealtime at home is a time of coming together to share with one another. In these busy times we rarely chat with our family members other than at meals. The conversation should be pleasant and interesting. Some subjects or unpleasant thoughts disrupt the digestive process. Avoid reference to anything "squeamish" or distasteful. It is rude to keep your eyes on the TV or an ear to the radio (or whatever other electronic device you may have) or your nose in the newspaper or a book. Some homes have a prayer after the meal or share a "precious promise" from God's Word.

Mealtime should be a happy time. It provides an opportunity to know and understand your family better and also to compliment the cook on the food, the table settings, or both.

Few homes have servants; Mother often has to play that role. Perhaps that is why going out to dinner is special to her. She deserves to be waited on once in a while. Grateful young people will assist in setting the table, serving, clearing the table, and cleaning up the kitchen. This goes for young men as well as young women. As the saying goes, "Many hands make light work."

The telephone

The way in which you answer the telephone tells the caller many things about you and your family. Your voice should have a smile in it. It shouldn't be harsh and abrasive, sickeningly sweet, or so soft no one can distinguish the words.

Start with a clear "Hello" and perhaps, "This is the Joneses' residence." If the call is for you, say, "This is she/he." If another person is wanted, you may say, "Just a moment, please." If the person asked for isn't there, simply say, "I'm sorry, he/she isn't here at the moment. Would you care to leave a message?" Or say, "I'll be happy to have him/her return your call." If the party called for is nearby, say, "Just a moment, I'll call her/him."

If you reach a wrong number when you dial, don't ask, "What number is this?" The party called may not want to disclose his/her number. You may ask, "Is this 555-7118?" for example, giving the number you wanted. If you receive a wrong number call, be gracious. Accept it as you would any mistake—with kindness.

Keep your conversation as short as possible, showing concern for the person you have called. He/she may have been in the middle of something important. It's wise to ask if you are calling at an inconvenient time so that the individual can be honest with you without fear of offending you. Ask if he/she would prefer you to call at another time.

If someone calls you at an inconvenient time, be frank and say that this is not a convenient time and you would be happy to return the call. If your voice is kind, your caller will respond with understanding.

Interruptions during a phone conversation may occur. If that happens, excuse yourself and offer to call later. It's rude to carry on a conversation with someone else while you are on the phone. Give the caller or the called party your undivided attention.

Except in an emergency or by prearrangement, don't call anyone early in the morning when people are often busy trying to get off to school or to work. Also, don't call someone after 9:30 P.M. unless you know the person and are sure that he/she has not retired for the night.

Don't use a company telephone, available through your job or someone else's, for personal calls. If there is an emergency, of course, use the company's phone, but keep the conversation brief. (See Appendix E: "Wally.")

Here are some other things to remember: keep your calls to a reasonable length of time; the caller should be the one to end the conversation; get permission to make toll calls and make arrangement for payment; and if you receive an obscene call, don't say anything—hang up and notify the telephone company.

Young people and phones seem to go together like hot dogs and cola. A telephone call can replace a visit, and you may be able to express yourself more freely. Also, it's often just plain fun! Just remember that sharing applies to the use of the telephone, too.

Your room—your castle!

How many times do young people say to their parents, "Oh, just shut the door; I'll take care of my room later"? In the meantime, Mother can't stand the sight of it, and out of frustration she cleans it for her procrastinating son or daughter.

Discipline and organization
are important rungs
on the ladder to maturity.

Failure to establish some routine for the appearance of your room only adds to a disorganized, undisciplined life.

Discipline and organization are important rungs on the ladder to maturity. If you allow yourself to be comfortable with clutter, other areas of your life will suffer from clutter as well.

If you share a room, work out a system that works well for both of you. This could be as simple as a second shelf in the closet (you may need a tiny stool if you can't stretch that tall) with a divider in the middle. All seldom-used or out-of-season items can be placed in a box (or boxes) and labeled. The second shelf can be divided with a brightly colored ribbon tied around the clothes rod at the center. Equal space is always a good idea, and it works for a desk and a chest of drawers, too. Space should not be divided on the basis of who owns more. Brothers and sisters can be competitive, jealous, and sometimes interfering, but practicing restraint and respect can eliminate much of the stress. Be fair and share the space.

Each day, make your bed and hang your clothes neatly (on hangers) in your closet. Keep long garments, such as robes, toward the back of the closet. Garments of a kind look much better when kept together—and they're much easier to find. (Closets can be beautiful if kept in order.) Place shoes in pairs, put dirty clothes in the hamper, and then stand back and admire your work!

Once a week you'll need to do some general cleaning to take care of the "fuzzies" that collect, and your furniture will need some dusting and perhaps a bit of a shine.

Your bedspread was probably selected with care to add to the decor of your room. Its newness will last if you remove it, or fold it back, while you're lounging. (See Appendix E: "Brad.")

If you keep books and records or a collection of some sort, arrange the items in an orderly fashion, and—presto!—you'll be able to find what you want when you want it! If need be, check to see if you could add another shelf. Perhaps you could talk Dad into a little carpentry work—another effort at togetherness for the family.

The bathroom

Gauge your time in the bathroom according to how many persons share it. It's a good idea to work out a morning schedule, giving priority to the one who has to leave home first.

Hot water may be in short supply, so use it sparingly. Some homes have septic systems that can't handle a lot of water at one time. Keep this in mind when you're under the shower.

Before you leave the bathroom, give it a quick check. Be sure that you have flushed the toilet and put the lid down. Putting the toilet lid down can save on costly plumbing repairs. Plumbers tell interesting stories of things retrieved from the toilet drain—everything from diamond rings to teddy bears!

Wipe up excess water, cap the toothpaste, fold the towels and, please, no hairs in the basin! If you used the tub, always clean it after your bath. A ring around the tub is disgusting and inexcusable. Wipe down the shower with a towel or sponge to eliminate film buildup and smelly mold. For extra measure, wipe off the chrome and keep it shining.

These little acts of consideration for others require only a few moments, but the rewards go on forever. Keep Philippians 2:3 in mind: *"Let each esteem others better than himself."* This takes care of selfishness.

Guests in the home

A vital part of family life is the entertaining of guests because that provides another opportunity to share and to learn. Guests bring a fresh, new feeling into the home, and everyone in the family can have a part in making them feel welcome. Having guests has always been considered a "special happening." Homes have been built with guest rooms, and shops are full of all sorts of little niceties for guests.

It's a compliment to your parents (and to you) to be considered good hosts, and for them to qualify, all family members, including the pets, will have to go a bit beyond the normal household procedures during the guests' visit. This can be a fun time for everyone. Most guests are friends of your parents, so be prepared to be patient while they discuss old times and friends. Parents like to show off their children, and this is your opportunity to shine for them.

Your parents will appreciate your help in tending to the following important items:

1. Have a comfortable bed ready for the guests, with extra blankets available. Bedpads are important for comfort and cleanliness.

2. Check the temperature of your home, especially in the guest room. If you turn the thermostat down to economize while you wear heavy sweaters to keep warm, your guests may be uncomfortable. Be sensitive to their comfort, or they may not return.

3. Have a reading lamp beside the bed. Some guests don't sleep well away from home and will appreciate being able to read.

4. Remove enough of your personal items from the closet, leaving plenty of hangers, so that room is provided for guests to hang their clothes.

5. If guests are to stay a week or more, provide an empty drawer. Make room on the tops of bureaus and chests for their personal items. It's wise to have a small, absorbent cloth or dresser scarf available to avoid stains from perfume and lotions. A small desk or a cleared space for writing a letter is another consideration your guests will appreciate.

6. Have plenty of soap (not all deodorant) and fresh, clean towels. Also, a little clock with an alarm is helpful. A guest room should have a chair; sitting on the bed is inconvenient and uncomfortable.

7. Give guests the privilege of retiring and rising when they desire. If breakfast must be served at a certain time, advise them, and they can prepare accordingly.
8. If at all possible, provide laundry facilities.
9. It cannot be stressed too much that your home, and especially the guest quarters, should be clean and without offensive odors.
10. Avoid forcing TV, games, or records on your guests. Be open to their ideas and suggestions of what to listen to and what to do.
11. If guests are not acquainted with your area of the country, offer some pleasant sight-seeing trips or activities. Your guests might enjoy getting to know some of your friends. Activities could be planned to include those opportunities, perhaps a swimming or a pizza party.
12. When entertaining your guests, be alert to any extra work created for your parents and lend a helping hand.
13. Guests should not be expected to help with household chores, but accept their offer graciously if they offer.
14. If guests overstay their visit, it will require tact to ask them to leave. Weigh the circumstances and be up-front and honest. They will thank you for it.

Many pet owners fail to realize that guests don't always share the affection they have for their pet. If you have pets, consider the possibility that your guests may feel uneasy around them or may be allergic to them. Unless your guests are genuine pet lovers, they will not appreciate having your animals paw them, rub against them, or otherwise ask for attention. Never allow pets to jump up on guests either in greeting or after guests are seated. As guests arrive, start to remove your pets from their presence. If they do not object to pets, you have given them an opportunity to say so.

It may not bother you for your pets to have free run of the kitchen or eat from your dishes, but guests could be offended. Keep pet dishes separated. Even dish cloths and towels can carry pet hairs to your tableware, so keep pets away from them. Dog or cat hairs in your guests' food are offensive and a sure way to prevent a return. Also, animal hairs can be transferred to guests' clothing from rugs or furniture. Keep both the animals and the furniture brushed regularly, and vacuum rugs whenever necessary.

A good host or hostess makes every effort to make a guest's stay a pleasant one. Friends are valuable, and life would be bleak without them. Cherish a good friendship and maintain it. True friends are for keeps!

"Distributing to the needs of the saints, given to hospitality" (Romans 12:13). *"Be hospitable to one another without grumbling"* (1 Peter 4:9).

Chapter 3

Challenges

1. Why are neatness and cleanliness important factors in the Christian life? Explain.

2. What positive steps can a young person take to develop an appreciation for parents' sentiment toward certain household items?

3. List ways in which teamwork can help create an orderly home.

4. Why are good table manners important in the home? Explain.

5. To show Christian hospitality in the home, what factors do you consider most important? Why?

6. List ways in which Christian principles can apply to telephone usage.

7. What suggestions can you give to family members who share a room?

8. How does selfishness affect a person's use of the home? Explain.

4

On Your Own —Away from Home

Next to your home and family, your school is probably the greatest influence on your life. You spend a lot of time there. Assuming there are 180 days in each school year, by graduation from high school you will have spent 15,120 hours in school.

School

Why is a school so important in your life? Because this is where knowledge is organized and presented to you. God has given you a great capacity for learning. It is possible for the human mind to store millions of separate items.

The Christian young person should have a thirst for knowledge. When you learn, you are storing up facts that will equip you for exciting opportunities that lie ahead. The class you consider a "bore" today may prove to be valuable to you someday.

Strive for high grades, not for the sake of grades alone but to support a Christian testimony. Pray for a retentive mind and a sharp intellect. God has a future planned for you, and you will need all the knowledge you can acquire.

Parents are aware of this fact and have selected the school you attend (be it a public or private school) not only for academic excellence but because they are assured that the school of their choice will provide the educational foundation you need for the college years that lie ahead. Christian schools are often selected because they are considered to be an extension of the home. The Christian school supports what parents believe and accept as important principles for living. Your school has a tremendous responsibility to live up to the faith and trust placed in it. Of course, no one person can make your school what you expect it to be. It takes the combined effort of students, faculty, administrators, and parents, plus—most important of all—wisdom from God.

"The fear of the Lord is the beginning of knowledge, but fools despise wisdom and instruction" (Proverbs 1:7). *"Happy is the man who finds wisdom, and the man who gains understanding"* (Proverbs 3:13). *"Wisdom is the principal thing; therefore get wisdom. And in all your getting, get understanding"* (Proverbs 4:7).

Schools must have rules. Most people resist rules, but all rules have a definite purpose. If you consider each rule individually—particularly the ones you object to most—you'll see clearly that all rules are for your safety, health, or general well-being. With a right attitude you can have fun and make valuable accomplishments within the limits of the school rules.

"Therefore let us pursue the things which make for peace" (Romans 14:19). *"And also if anyone competes in athletics, he is not crowned unless he competes according to the rules"* (2 Timothy 2:5).

Along with the administrators and faculty, you want to be proud of your school. Making it the best requires teamwork, cooperation, and respect for those in authority over you. You are being watched by children in the lower grades. You are an example to them, for good or for not-so-good.

"For I have given you an example, that you should do as I have done to you" (John 13:15).

At school, with people all around you, you can polish

Hold high the torch!
You did not light its glow—
'Twas given you by other hands, you know.
'Tis yours to keep it burning bright,
Yours to pass on when you no more need light;
For there are other feet that we must guide,
And other forms go marching by our side;
Their eyes are watching every smile and tear,
And efforts which we think are not worthwhile
Are sometimes just the very helps they need,
Actions to which their souls would give most heed;
So that in turn they'll hold it high
And say, "I watched someone else carry it this way."

If brighter paths should beckon you to choose,
Would your small gain compare with all you'd lose?
Hold high the torch!
You did not light its glow—
'Twas given you by other hands, you know,
I think it started down its pathway bright
The day the Maker said: "Let there be light."
And He once said, who hung on Calvary's tree—
    "Ye are the light of the world."
      . . . Go! . . . Shine—for me.

—Author Unknown

the manners you've learned. Also, you'll be helping your school become a display of true Christian behavior.

Work at keeping the building clean and orderly. Discourage carelessness in other students. Don't run in the halls or obstruct them by standing or walking in groups. Always keep to the right when walking in the crowded halls and on the stairs. Reserve your yelling and loud noises for outdoors or the sports arena, being mindful that others in the building may still be having class. Hold doors so they won't close in the face of someone behind you.

It may be difficult, but exercise patience while standing in line. Lines go with schools; you can't avoid them, whether it is at the drinking fountain or waiting to enter the auditorium. Don't push or shove. That is rude. Moreover, pushing and shoving can cause a serious accident. Such behavior reflects selfishness and ingratitude in the strictest sense and has no place in the life of a Christian young person.

Visitors may be a frequent sight in your school. Smile at them, and be polite and prompt to offer assistance or directions to the school office. The kindness and consideration you show to visitors will speak well for you and your school. Your courteousness is a great advertisement for your school.

Our Lord dignified the role of teacher. He was often addressed with the title *rabbi,* which means "honorable teacher." Teachers are human beings who have spent years in training for this role. They deserve your respect. It would be interesting to know why they became teachers. Most would tell you that they enjoy working with young people and their greatest reward is to know they have helped them. Did you ever wonder what kind of teacher assumed the responsibility of teaching Helen Keller, who was without sight and hearing? How thrilled she was when her pupil was able to say, ever so slowly, "wa-ter."

Address your teacher as "Miss," "Mr.," "Mrs.," "Ms.," "Dr.," or "Sister." It's disrespectful to say "Teacher" or use only the last name. Don't argue with your teacher or publicly challenge any statements he/she makes. If there is a difference of opinion on a sensitive subject or one that could provoke an argument, speak privately to him/her. This is not to say, however, that you can't express an opinion; that's what class discussion is all about. Weigh what you are about to say, and make it constructive. Class discussion provides valuable insights into how others feel and can be informative as well. What you contribute can make it even more interesting.

Many classrooms are classics of disarray. Not all teachers are good room keepers, but this is no excuse for you to participate in that pattern. Keep your own area in order, conducive to good study habits. Be an example. Sit only on chairs, never on desks. The teacher's desk is private property; nothing on it should be touched.

Good citizenship can be learned and practiced in the classroom. Be sensitive to classmates who have special needs or problems. Some may have handicaps. Be prompt to assist when needed. Show them that you care.

In most schools cliques are formed. However, cliques often cause severe damage to students who already have low self-images. It hurts to be left out or ignored. Cliques discriminate against and alienate others. Hostility will result from such practices and hinder an atmosphere for learning. The small, thoughtful, kind acts that you perform label you as a person who is nice to have around. A reputation lasts a long time. You have probably heard that a good reputation can open the door, but a bad reputation will shut the door in your face. Allow Christ to shine through you in your relationships.

Many of the friends you make at school will become lifelong friends. There is a closeness that develops as you share with one another those growing-up experiences with their joys and tears.

To get the most from your school years, keep a positive attitude and get involved in school activities. There's a place for everyone. Support school projects by lending a hand wherever needed. If your school has a fund-raising project, get in there and give it all you've got. Go over the top and encourage your friends to do the same. Remember, it's your school!

"A man who has friends must himself be friendly" (Proverbs 18:24).

Assemblies

Rudeness and immaturity often come to full bloom in the auditorium or assembly hall. Some students seem to make a contest out of who can be the loudest or attract the most attention. It may be difficult for the teacher to keep control as students mingle with other groups and classes. Students must exercise responsibility for their own behavior.

Assembly speakers or artists are your guests and should be given full respect. This includes giving your attention to them during their talks or presentations. If a speaker does not catch your interest, try to figure out why, and tuck it away in a cubbyhole in your mind to be used on that day when you are a speaker somewhere. It could happen, and you will be grateful for this learning experience!

Applause improperly used can be a hindrance. The purpose of applause is to compliment a speaker or performer. It's a collective way of saying, "Thank you." Under no circumstances should there be whistling, rhythmic clapping, or foot stomping. (Marching soldiers have to "break step" when crossing a bridge because the pressure created by rhythm can be disastrous. A great hotel balcony crumbled, killing and injuring many guests, because of the pressure generated by music and dancing, for instance.)

Use your assembly time for learning. The administrators must have considered this time of bringing the students together to be a worthwhile experience. You can trust them!

Uniforms

If your school requires uniforms, wear yours with pride. Keep it clean and pressed. Be sure to mend it when necessary, also. Uniforms serve several purposes, some of which are encouraging neatness in appearance; eliminating the high cost of clothing, as well as clothes consciousness; fostering good behavior; and establishing a fair dress code.

It has been proven psychologically that what you wear affects your behavior. A prestigious boys' school in New England refused to give in to the pressure to alter a dress code that required shirts, ties, and sports coats. The school expected high scholastic achievement of each student, and the discipline that comes with a dress code was necessary for high achievement. They had proven it through the years.

At church

Technically speaking, the church is God's people, Christ's Bride. But here we want to consider our behavior while we are in the building or room that is set aside for religious services, the place we usually call "church." Services have a threefold purpose, namely, to praise God, to worship God, and to learn of God. These purposes were set forth by Scripture and have been observed for centuries.

What you wear affects your behavior.

"Blessed are those who dwell in Your house; they will still be praising you. Selah" (Psalm 84:4). *"And were continually in the temple praising and blessing God"* (Luke 24:53; see also John 7:14; Acts 2:46; 3:1). *"And they worshiped Him, and returned to Jerusalem with great joy"* (Luke 24:52). *"Many nations shall come and say, 'Come, and let*

us go up to the mountain of the Lord, to the house of the God of Jacob; He will teach us His ways, and we shall walk in His paths'" (Micah 4:2).

Through reverence to God, some basic patterns for behavior and dress developed. Although we know that God looks at the heart, we also see that God has an eye for beauty, design, and appropriateness as we read His instructions for the building of the tabernacle in Exodus 25:8–9: *"And let them make Me a sanctuary, that I may dwell among them. According to all that I show you, that is, the pattern of the tabernacle and the pattern of all its furnishings, just so you shall make it."* The design included shittim wood (from a special tree grown only in the Middle East), pure gold, beaten (hammered) work, cherubs, silver, badger skins, fine twined linen, solid brass, and colors of blue, purple, and scarlet.

Reverence is the key to our behavior in church. *"God is greatly to be feared in the assembly of the saints, and to be held in reverence by all those around Him"* (Psalm 89:7). If our attitude upon entering the church is that we are coming into the presence of a sovereign God, instructions on how to behave would be unnecessary. In recent times, though, many of us seem to have removed God from His throne and reduced Him to mediocrity or a "nice guy" with whom anything goes. Much of our lifestyle has been reduced to mediocrity anyway, but it is unfortunate that the anything-goes attitude enters a sanctuary dedicated to the God of our redemption.

"Let all the earth fear the Lord; let all the inhabitants of the world stand in awe of Him" (Psalm 33:8). *"You shall keep My Sabbaths and reverence My sanctuary: I am the Lord"* (Leviticus 19:30).

With these thoughts in mind, enter the church quietly and reverently. A young man should remove his topcoat in the vestibule and place it on a coatrack or in a cloakroom, as provided. A young woman may keep her coat, but she shouldn't drape it over the pew in front of her. If you are late, wait for a break in the service when an usher can direct you to a seat. If a young man and a young woman are together, the young woman follows the usher with her escort following. If there is no usher, the young man leads to the pew, stands aside allowing the young woman to enter, and then takes a seat beside her. The young woman always enters the pew first, and the young man follows. Don't climb over people. It's courteous to move over and make room for latecomers.

Whispering, giggling, chewing gum, or reading anything that is not related to the service is rude and inconsiderate. Also, any display of affection or touching is in very poor taste. Hymnbooks should be returned to the racks after use. All chatting with friends should be done after the service, at the back of the sanctuary or in the vestibule so as not to disturb some who might desire to remain to pray or speak to the minister. Remember the threefold purpose for which you attend church—to praise God, to worship God, and to learn of God. Correct behavior will then be natural to you.

Most churches have a midweek service that you may want to attend and it isn't necessary to dress in your Sunday best. However, no service held in a church is a casual occasion, and you should dress accordingly. Clothing worn to a picnic or an athletic game is obviously inappropriate. The clothing you choose to wear reflects an attitude, and what you wear to church should reflect an attitude of respect for God.

"Let it be the hidden person of the heart, with the incorruptible beauty of a gentle and quiet spirit, which is very precious in the sight of God" (1 Peter 3:4).

"A woman shall not wear anything that pertains to a man, nor shall a man put on a woman's garment, for all who do so are an abomination to the Lord your God" (Deuteronomy 22:5).

In recent days, applause has become a problem for the clergy. Primarily, it disrupts a spirit of worship. Also, applause is basically a thank-you to the performer, and your minister doesn't desire to be considered a performer. Musicians are also worshiping God through their music and are not performers in the church. No hard and fast rule can be made, but in most instances it's best to refrain from applause. In the event applause is requested, then, of course, you oblige and applaud with the congregation.

Regarding the minister, address him as "Doctor" Jones if he has a doctor's degree. If not, use the title "Mr." Jones or "Pastor" Jones. Never address him as just "Reverend." "Reverend Mr. Jones" is also correct, although very formal. Addressing a minister by his first name indicates a lack of recognition of his divine authority over the congregation. Ministers are called apart to serve the people of the congregation as undershepherds. (The Shepherd, of course, is Christ Himself.) We are commanded to respect them both in title and in attitude.

"Receive him therefore in the Lord with all gladness, and hold such men in esteem" (Philippians 2:29). *"Esteem them very highly in love for their work's sake"* (1 Thessalonians 5:13). *"Let the elders who rule well be counted worthy of double honor, especially those who labor in the word and doctrine"* (1 Timothy 5:17).

Here are some guidelines to help you:
- Be on time.
- Be friendly.
- Bring your Bible.
- Sit reasonably toward the front.
- Join in the congregational singing.
- Follow the reading of the Scriptures.
- Enter into the time of prayer.
- Listen attentively and respectfully to those who are speaking or singing.
- Refrain from talking during the service.
- Don't pass notes.
- Don't read Sunday school papers.
- Take notes on the sermon. (This is good mental discipline.)

- Turn to the Scripture passages and follow along with the minister.
- Examine your life in the light of the truth presented and ask yourself—"How can I apply this truth to my life personally?"
- Sit quietly during a closing invitation to accept Christ so as not to disturb individuals pondering a decision.
- Be a doer of the Word—follow through with the promise or vow you made to the Lord.

Church-sponsored activities provide excellent opportunities for Christian growth and involvement. You will be with young people who share your views and interests. Parents feel comfortable, too, about saying yes to weekend retreats. They appreciate Christian concern, leadership, and chaperoning.

Churches need your involvement. Nothing makes a pastor's heart rejoice more than to see his young people actively participating in church activities. You add that special kind of encouragement.

If you feel there isn't much going on for youth in your church, use your ingenuity and organize some youth projects, such as car washes, clean-up-the-church day, trips to nursing homes and hospitals, song times after church—the list is endless. You will be developing your own leadership abilities; at the same time He will be pleased and will give you multiple blessings. You can count on it!

Weddings

If you are attending a church wedding, wait at the back of the center aisle (or designated aisle) for an usher. He will ask you if you are a friend of the bride or the groom. The bride's guests are seated on the right and the groom's on the left as you face the front of the church.

As the usher offers his arm, a young woman takes his arm and is escorted down the aisle. If a young man is with her, he follows behind. If a young man is alone, he walks beside the usher.

When the wedding party enters, it is correct to turn and watch. When the service is over, remain seated in the pew until the bridal party and family have departed.

The bride's mother is usually first in the receiving line. If you don't know her, introduce yourself. Remember to keep moving. Don't stop to chat. Wish the bride happiness and congratulate the groom.

Follow the guests to the reception table. Receive the food graciously and move away from the table. Your cue to leave the reception is when the bride and groom leave the reception.

Funerals

When you are made aware of the death of a friend or an acquaintance, be prompt with sympathetic gestures. It's never easy to comfort the bereaved, but any gesture of kindness is appreciated in a time of sorrow. Some ways in which to convey your sympathy are a note, food delivered to the home, or an offer to perform some needed tasks, such as picking up cleaning, polishing shoes, fixing meals, washing dishes, looking after small children, taking care of pets, and so forth. To a close friend, a touch or a gentle hug speaks volumes. A sudden death can bring confusion, and many needs arise. Saying, "If there's anything I can do, just phone me," is meaningless. If you look closely, you will see many needs and opportunities to help meet those needs. You'll always be happy that you were there to help.

If you are close friends of the family, make a personal call prior to the funeral. If your family is bereaved, try to make the guests feel at ease. Guests often feel like intruders at such a time.

When you call at a funeral home, observe the hours. Usually someone from the family is there to greet you. Stay only as long as appears appropriate, and remember to offer your sympathy. If you have committed Scriptures to memory, an appropriate verse spoken to the bereaved is often helpful and eases an awkward situation. You aren't obligated to stop beside the casket. If you do, a brief pause or silent prayer to the family is appropriate. Speak with others briefly, sign the guest register, and depart.

Attending the funeral is a tribute of respect to the family. If there are ushers, walk beside the usher. (A young woman does not take his arm as she does at a wedding.) If there are no ushers, seat yourself quietly.

Your dress should be conservative. Tradition dictates the dress of the bereaved to be dark. The mourning period is considered to be six months to a year, and during that time, the bereaved, in respect to the deceased, refrain from parties and gala celebrations. This, of course, is a matter of personal preference.

If you send flowers, send them to the funeral home. Close friends may send small bouquets to the home as well. This thoughtful act says, "I love you. I care." Flowers can be sent by individuals or groups. In some instances, a memorial gift is requested in lieu of flowers. The "in lieu" notice usually appears in the local newspaper, and the request is expected to be observed by all except, perhaps, a very close friend or relative. A check is sent to the charity with a note saying the donation is given in (loving) memory of the deceased (name). The family of the deceased should acknowledge gifts with a personal note.

Public places

Now that you are approaching adulthood, you'll find that your public life will make more demands of you, and personal discipline is required to meet those demands. If, however, your parents required you from an early age to be conscious of the image you project, your public role will not be as difficult as it might have been without that previous experience.

Courtesy is expressed in every socially correct rule. In a public place, make an effort to be inconspicuous. This, of course, rules out laughing loudly, calling to someone across a room or on the street, or whistling. Also, you shouldn't eat or drink while walking or standing in a public place. Gum chewing is for private places, too.

"Your word I have hidden in my heart, that I might not sin against You" (Psalm 119:11). *"Your word is a lamp to my feet and a light to my path"* (Psalm 119:105). *"I have inclined my heart to perform Your statutes forever, to the very end"* (Psalm 119:112).

On the street

Throughout Scripture, God ordained man to be the head of the woman. *"Then the rib which the Lord God had taken from man He made into a woman, and He brought her to the man"* (Genesis 2:22). *"But I want you to know that the head of every man is Christ, the head of woman is man, and the head of Christ is God"* (1 Corinthians 11:3).

Tradition has supported this chain-of-command concept. It has been only in recent years with the emergence of the demand for equal rights that the concept has been challenged. Correct behavior, however, still holds that the man should take the leading (and protective) role when with a woman.

When a young man and a young woman meet on the street, the young woman should speak first, and the young man returns the greeting. If they are crossing a street together, she may take his arm as he offers it. He shouldn't cup his hand and place it under her elbow or guide her with his arm. He should walk on the curb side of the street. This custom evolved from the day when it was feared that runaway horses might run onto the sidewalk. A man was expected (and still is) to protect his companion.

If a young man is walking with two young women, he should walk on one side of them so that he doesn't have to keep turning his head from side to side as they walk and talk. If there are more than three people to walk abreast, they should divide and walk two by two.

A young man should offer to assist a young woman carrying a heavy article, such as a suitcase or a bag of groceries. This is a courtesy that he extends to her.

Stairs

The young woman usually goes down the stairs first, unless the steps are steep and treacherous, in which case the young man goes before her. On an escalator, there is no established rule, but the young man usually goes first and offers assistance as the young woman enters. He steps from the escalator first, again offering his hand (always palm up) to assist.

Doors

A young woman approaches the door first and stands aside so the young man can open it for her. If it is a swinging door or one that pushes in, he may go first and hold it for her. A young man should be prompt to open a door. If he is too slow, an awkward situation may arise.

Elevators

A young woman enters an elevator first and exits first, unless male passengers are nearest the door. They step off when the elevator stops rather than step aside for the young woman to get off. If a young woman is with a young man and both are standing near the rear of the elevator, he steps off the elevator first and waits for her.

A young man does not remove his hat in a business elevator (in an office building, for example) but does remove his hat on a private elevator (in an apartment building). Also, he allows her to exit first in a private elevator.

Taxis and other means of transportation

A young woman precedes a young man into a taxi and moves to the farthest corner to make room for her escort or other passengers. If a young woman is alone, she should sit on the right-hand side of the rear seat. A young man gets out of a taxi first and then assists the young woman, or women, by offering his hand.

If you are on a date, the young man pays the cab fare. If the fare is shared, one person pays the bill, and the settling up is done after leaving the cab.

A young man should assist a young woman out of a car. If he is the driver, he should get out and open the door for her. In today's busy world, this act of graciousness is often ignored. However, it is always appreciated, and a man is respected for it.

On a bus, subway, or train, the young woman enters first. A young man should give up his seat to an elderly woman or man, a person carrying a child, or an expectant

---

Be conscious of the social rights of others.

---

mother. A young woman, too, should offer her seat to someone who appears to need it more than she does. This gesture of kindness is too often neglected. Unless it's a date, a young woman pays for her own fare. It's correct for the young man to make inquiries about transfers and so on.

"And be kind to one another" (Ephesians 4:32).

When you are with a companion or companions in a public place, stay together. It is never wise (or safe) to wander off alone, or even in twos, in a strange place. Keep in mind also that you are on exhibit. Be conscious of the social rights of others, and show courtesy to them and to your companions (a good place to follow the golden rule). Rudeness in public places may have become almost a national pastime, but you as a Christian shouldn't contribute to it.

When you are with a date in a public place, adopt a hands-off policy. Holding hands or cuddling is inappropriate and offensive to others. Kissing in public, except a good-bye or greeting at a transportation departure or arrival point, is taboo. Remember, a good-bye kiss is just that, not a long embrace.

Galleries, museums, national monuments

At galleries and museums, certain restrictions and observances are required. These are usually posted, or the guide will explain them to you. Listen attentively as the guide talks about the exhibits. If you don't have an advantageous position, don't push ahead or step in front of others. Usually groups move from one spot to another, and you will be given another opportunity to be in the line of "sight and sound." Here, too, stay with your original companions. Don't wander off!

Galleries, museums, and national monuments, whether at home or abroad, are important to each country's heritage. They belong to the people and are provided for interest and information. All the rules of courtesy and respect apply. Although no one is going to prescribe a code of dress at such places, the wise Christian young person will be sensitive to what is appropriate and will dress and behave accordingly, showing the respect due.

Going to a party

When you are invited to a party, you should acknowledge the invitation by telephone or note. If you accept, you obligate yourself to be on time and dressed appropriately.

If you want to be invited again, you should try to add to the fun, be helpful when needed, and be both interested and interesting. The food table may be inviting, but take modest portions and move away from the table. If you are with a date be attentive and assist each other, especially in a serve-yourself arrangement. You may return to the table if you wish, but remember—modest portions!

If no plates are provided, only napkins, be careful where you set your cup or glass. Do not place used cups or glasses on the food table nor on the furniture. If a place for used cups, plates, and napkins is not obvious, ask your host or hostess.

Mingle with the other guests and introduce yourself to those you do not know (if the host or hostess has overlooked an introduction). If you go with a date, stay with your date but include other guests in your conversation. Keep the conversation light and avoid discussions that cannot be shared by those near you. Leave the party at the closing time indicated by the host or hostess.

If it is a birthday party, the invitation will probably indicate if a gift is expected. If the invitation says, "no gifts, please," that request should be honored. If the invitation is by phone, the caller should indicate if gifts will be given. If not, ask.

Afternoon tea

Afternoon teas are becoming more popular for both young men and young women. Should you be invited to one, go during the time specified on your invitation but not later than twenty minutes before the close. Dress appropriately. Sportswear isn't appropriate. Young men should always wear a jacket and tie.

After you are greeted by your hostess and have left your wraps in a designated place, you may move from group to group. Go to the table for refreshments, unless they are being brought to the guests. Move away from the table as soon as possible. You may sit or stand. In either position, completely unfold the tea napkin and keep it in your lap or under the plate you are holding.

The length of your stay should usually be about thirty minutes. If a young woman has gone to the tea with a young man, she is the one to suggest leaving. The young man should get the wraps. After both of you thank your hostess, you should leave promptly.

Being a guest

"Be hospitable to one another without grumbling" (1 Peter 4:9).

At some time you'll be a guest in someone's home—the home of a friend, friends of your parents, or perhaps relatives. There are some very special rules for you to remember, and all of them are based on courtesy and consideration.

As the number of people in a home increases, some necessary adjustments must be made. The work load also increases with more cooking, dishes, and laundry. Some individuals may have special diets to observe that require planning. It would be unfair for this added responsibility to rest solely upon the hostess. Everyone should share in the work, including you.

Prior to your visit, inquire about the weather and planned activities, and pack only what is needed. Your host and hostess will probably not welcome a car trunk full of suitcases, armfuls of garments, or multiple boxes of shoes. If closet space is limited (and it usually is), your belongings will only clutter their home.

If you know prior to your visit what activities are planned (a camping trip or a few days in the city) and the length of your stay, your packing will be quite simple. Make a list of all the things you think you will need and then go over that list a few times to see what can be eliminated. Most of us take along much more than we actually need. Consider, for instance, whether you will need dressy clothes for church or a special social event.

When you arrive, accept the accommodations offered. Use the closet space and drawers provided for you. Keep personal items, such as toothpaste, hair spray, perfume, and other toiletries, in your suitcase or travel bag. Don't place them on furniture. Many beautiful dresser tops have been ruined by the alcohol content of some cosmetics. Luggage is placed on the floor or on a luggage rack, never on the bed. Bedspreads and coverlets are costly and often are dry cleanable only.

The routine of the household will become obvious, so make every effort to adjust. Ask your hostess to suggest a time to arise. Sleeping beyond that time is taboo. Be careful not to put any extra work on your hostess. Keep your room neat, make your bed, and hang towels neatly.

Be aware of others who use the bath, and limit your time. Many homes are on septic systems and wells. Remember—no long showers or tubs full of water.

Offer assistance to your host and hostess whenever possible, and show your appreciation with sincere thank-you's. Don't expect anyone to wait on you.

Leave at the planned time, and be prompt with a thank-you note as soon as you reach home or your next stopping place.

Traveling

The better you plan, the better the trip will be. As mentioned earlier, take a minimum of clothing. If you plan well, deciding what to take won't be a problem. If you can, color coordinate your clothing. If you are traveling in winter and your outercoat is brown, for instance, take accessories and clothing to go with brown. If you are traveling in summer, the same idea about color coordination applies, but your colors should be lighter. Conservative clothing can have multiple uses, and it cuts down on luggage.

Decide with your parents on the amount of money you should take, and carry travelers' checks and credit cards (if you have them). Keep cash to a minimum and in a safe place. Young women should keep handbags close and in sight at all times. Although you may never have an encounter with a purse snatcher, there are such people. A money belt is a good idea. A suitcase is *not* a safe place—luggage may get lost or stolen. Have necessary telephone numbers and your family credit card number (if you have one) along with you.

If you are traveling abroad, guard your passport as if your life depended upon it—it almost does. A lost passport creates a multitude of problems and delays. Should the worst happen and you lose your passport, contact the nearest American Embassy. It is advisable to have some local currency (of the country you visit) in small bills and change when you arrive.

Make reservations (they are free) either by calling the carrier's office directly (plane, bus, train) or by making arrangements through a travel agent. If you have to cancel, do it promptly. Someone else may be able to use the seat you reserved. Check the allowed weight of the baggage and the size limit. If a porter helps you, remember that he expects a tip (usually fifty cents a bag).

If you have your ticket and are running late, check your baggage with a porter at the curb (again, fifty cents per bag). He can arrange to get your luggage to your plane faster than you can by standing in line at the check-in counter.

Obey the signs at the front of the cabin (if traveling by air) and all signs that light up en route. These are for your safety and protection. Rest rooms are provided on all public carriers except, perhaps, small commuter planes.

Meals are sometimes provided, and on planes you'll be served at your seat. No tip is given to in-flight personnel. On trains, someone will come through announcing that "dinner is served." Dinner on a train is usually expensive, so be prepared. You order and tip just as in any nice restaurant (about 15 percent of the bill).

Keep conversation impersonal, and don't accept gifts or hospitality from strangers. Be careful not to give out information about where you'll be staying or the names of the people you'll be visiting. Caution is always the best policy.

Traveling often presents opportunities to present Christ and the Christian message. Exercise all the courtesies you know: be sensitive to the interests and responses of the person with whom you are speaking. Present, but don't force your views or conversation.

If you are going to be staying in a hotel, you may be provided transportation to that hotel by its special limousine, which is less expensive than a taxi. However, you may have to take a taxi instead. There are usually plenty of them at the point of arrival, but be sure the taxi is a well-known carrier and not an independent. National companies usually make an effort to adhere to consistent policies of safety and integrity. It isn't wise to travel via taxi alone.

Hotel and motel reservations are generally held only until 6:00 P.M. If you will be arriving later, notify the hotel prior to the deadline. Hotels and motels can be expensive, so be sure you have this information in hand before making a reservation. Most hotels do not allow pets. It is advisable to ask prior to arrival.

You should receive a confirmation of your reservation from your travel agent or the hotel. If your reservation has been prepaid, you should receive a receipt prior to departure. If a mistake has been made, it is much easier to correct prior to your arrival. When you register, be sure the price you are being charged agrees with the price on the confirmation and that it is the room that was assigned to you.

All guests must register. It's a law. But one person can sign for all family members. It's permissible to ask to see the room before you accept it. If it's not to your liking, you may ask for another or decide to leave. Ask about check-out time. If you stay over your time, you may have to pay for another day. Instead, use the baggage checkroom and pay that fee (usually small) when you are leaving the area after check-out time.

In a hotel, a bellhop will carry your luggage to your room. For this service he expects a tip (usually fifty cents a bag). At a motel, the desk clerk usually gives you a key, and you are on your own. The clerk is not tipped, but the maid who cleans your room may be, if you choose, when your stay extends beyond two or three days. (See appendix D, "Tipping.")

Acquaint yourself with the location of the fire escapes and the exit. Consult your room directory for hotel services. Security is very important, so keep your door double locked and chained at all times. Make sure your sliding glass doors and windows are locked, too. If you leave your room only for a few moments to get ice or a cold drink, lock your door behind you. Most doors have peepholes through which you can see a caller. Do *not* open your door without knowing who is calling.

Hotels offer various eating options, such as (a) *American Plan:* room accommodations with three meals daily [in other countries it may be called *Full Pension* or *Full Board*]; (b) *Modified American Plan:* room accommodations and breakfast with one other meal—lunch or dinner [in other countries it may be called *Demi Pension* or *Half Board*]; (c) *Continental Plan:* room accommodations with a continental breakfast—coffee, tea, or milk with rolls, butter, and jam; (d) *Bermuda Plan:* room accommodations with a full American-style breakfast—usually including juice, fruit, eggs, meat, and Danish pastry; (e) *Á la Carte:* a menu from which you may make a number of selections; and (f) *Table d'Hôte:* a fixed menu.

Don't leave any valuables in your room. Most hotels provide safety deposit boxes for their guests. Treat the room and

all furnishings with respect. Don't iron on the furniture.
Most hotels and motels can provide an ironing board upon
request.

Again, wherever you are, when traveling with companions, stay with them!

The family car

Most states permit young people to drive at age sixteen.
Passing a driver's test and being issued a license is an exciting
experience and a giant step toward maturity.

With this experience, however, comes some awesome responsibilities. Not only are you responsible for your own
safety, you are responsible for the safety of those who ride
with you as well as the pedestrians on the street and the oc-
cupants of other vehicles.

If your parents respect your maturity enough to allow
you the use of the family car, pay close attention and observe
all the conditions they set for the use of the car. Parents pay a
high insurance premium for driving privileges for their children who are under the age of twenty-one. If you want this
privilege to continue, it's only fair to earn it.

Summer camp

Many young people are given the opportunity to go to
summer camp. There are Christian youth camps for the purpose of building the Christian life as well as baseball camps,
tennis camps, foreign language camps, equestrian camps,
and many others. All of them provide learning experiences
with other youths of similar interests in a beautiful outdoor
setting.

Camping is a fun opportunity for young people to live
together in dormitories or in tents and eat in dining halls.
Camp fire sing-alongs, hiking and boating trips, nature walks,
and swimming meets are just a few of the activities. Warm

and lasting friendships develop as young people from various backgrounds and economic levels come together for times of sharing and learning.

But all camps have rules, and because of the responsibility and state regulations placed on the camp directors, the rules have to be rigidly enforced. Don't ask for special favors or consideration. Study the camp brochure before registering. Be prepared to obey the rules and to have a great time with a host of new friends.

Baby-sitting

To accept a job as a baby-sitter is to accept a high honor. There is no possession so valuable as one's child. To be trusted and considered capable to care for a child is indeed an honor. But with honor comes responsibility.

You are a specialist. You have been called on to care for a child. Pay attention to all instructions provided and follow them closely. Be sure to have your duties explained clearly; you shouldn't be expected to do household chores. If the child is sleeping and you can give attention to some small task while still keeping a watchful eye, it would be gracious and kind of you. However, your function as a baby-sitter is to attend the child, which does include picking up toys and keeping the home tidy.

Have a list of telephone numbers available in case of an emergency. You should have the following numbers: police, fire department, the place where the parents are for the evening, a reliable friend or a relative to advise in case of emergency, the child's doctor, and the hospital. Don't use the phone for making or receiving personal calls.

You are the one asked to baby-sit. Don't invite a friend. Help yourself to food and beverages only if invited to do so. Make previous arrangements to get home safely, either with the parents you are baby-sitting for or with your own parents.

The job interview

Job interviews are a natural part of life. Keep in mind that the employer or interviewer is also a human being and has probably experienced the same fright and apprehension that you feel.

Of course, you will be anxious. You want the job, and the responsibility of convincing the employer that you are the one for the job rests on you. With the right attitude and adherence to a few basic principles, your tension will be relieved, and success will be yours.

The United States Department of Labor conducted a survey to determine the twelve skills needed most for success on the job. A basic knowledge of these skills will be of great benefit to you. They are (1) giving an honest day's work, (2) recognizing your strengths and weaknesses, (3) getting along with others, (4) being a team member, (5) basic writing and speaking skills, (6) understanding written information, (7) maintaining good health, (8) organizing the work activities of others, (9) maintaining a clean and neat appearance, (10) being punctual, (11) being dependable, and (12) having a sense of humor.

Let's begin with your appearance. Make sure that you are clean and neat and that your clothing is well pressed. How you wear your hair is important, especially if the job is in food service. Employers shy away from applicants whose hair is "dust mop" style or long and shaggy. Hair in food is a colossal problem and a sure way to ruin a business. Research on young male executives has proven that employers tend to choose the clean-shaven applicant over those with facial hair. Finally, have a nice smile revealing clean teeth and breath.

Dress appropriately. If you are applying for a job in a business office, reason dictates a jacket and tie for a young man, a suit or tailored dress (perhaps a skirt and blouse) for a young woman. A young woman should avoid slacks. Jeans are taboo for either sex unless the job calls for manual labor, such as working in a garage or doing lawn maintenance. Whatever the clothing, fit is important, not tight and revealing or loose and baggy. Young women should avoid sleeveless dresses or blouses.

Jewelry should be simple. It is better to wear too little jewelry than too much. Young women must use good taste in makeup, also. Too much makeup or makeup poorly applied may suggest a person that really isn't you. Cosmetic departments of some stores can give good makeup assistance, with usually only a small purchase required.

Before you go to your interview, find out anything you can about the company. Prior knowledge of the size and interests of the business, for instance, or any other details can be valuable as you answer the interviewer's questions.

Be punctual! Arriving on time, with a few minutes to spare, is essential to the good impression you want to make in this interview. Every employer appreciates punctuality for itself and for the character it shows.

Have all necessary papers with you, including your working permit if you are under the age of eighteen. Fill out all forms and applications correctly and neatly. Have names, addresses, and phone numbers of references and former employers on hand. The appearance of your paperwork is almost as important as your personal appearance.

When you are invited into the office where the interview will take place, greet the employer or interviewer by name and sit in the seat offered to you. Relax—try not to fumble with something in your hands. Keep your attention on the matter at hand. Be careful not to touch anything on the employer's desk. It's advisable to decline refreshment (coffee or cold drinks) to avoid any accidents or fumbling. Remember—no gum chewing!

Be pleasant and answer questions honestly and politely. Don't volunteer too much information. The interviewer knows what he/she is looking for and will ask for it. Look directly at the interviewer when you respond to questions.

Allow the employer to tell you about the job; if you have questions about it, ask them. You have a right to know what would be expected of you, and it is better to ask now than later. Employers are generally very busy people, so keep to the point.

When the interviewer pushes his chair back and begins to stand, that is your cue to go. He will probably thank you for coming and tell you that you will be hearing from him. Thank him sincerely and depart.

A job interview can be a pleasant learning experience and is one more step on the road to mature, responsible adulthood.

To complete a job application

Answer all items on an application form honestly, accurately, and completely. Fill in all items by printing in ink as neatly as possible. Plan your answers before you print them. Read all instructions carefully. If an item doesn't apply to you, write *N.A.* to stand for the words *Not Applicable*. Be sure your finished application represents the kind of work you want to do for your prospective employer—as neat and exact as you can make it. See the sample application form for Chick-fil-A.

Money

Allowances depend on how much parents can afford and how much responsibility the young person can handle. There is no set rule as to how much an allowance should be, or even if there should be one at all.

It is important that a young person be considerate of the family's financial responsibilities and understand the importance of living within one's means. The earlier in life this lesson is learned, the more successful one will be in handling

Chick-fil-A Trademark ®

APPLICATION FOR EMPLOYMENT   *All Information Treated Confidentially*

Name (print) _____ Date _____
                   FIRST   MIDDLE   LAST

People Call Me " _____ " Home Phone No. _____ Soc. Sec. No. _____
                        NAME

Present Address _____
                   NO.   STREET   CITY   STATE   ZIP CODE

In case of Emergency
please notify _____ Address _____ Phone _____

What wage are you expecting? _____ If you are younger than 18 years old, how old are you? _____

Are you eligible to work in the U.S.A.? YES _____ NO _____ Have you ever been convicted of a felony? _____ YES _____ NO

Why are you seeking employment with Chick-fil-A? _____
_____

How were you referred to Chick-fil-A? _____

AVAILABILITY

When will you be available?

					M	T	W	Th	Fr	Sat
All Year	Yes _____ No _____		Check	Morning						
School Year	Yes _____ No _____	Total Hours	Days And	Afternoon						
Summer	Yes _____ No _____	You Want To	Time Of Day	Evening						
Other _____		Work Per Week _____	Available							

PREVIOUS EMPLOYMENT HISTORY

Have you ever worked at a Chick-fil-A restaurant before? If yes, dates and location _____

List 3 most recent jobs:

DATES EMPLOYED FROM TO	NAME & ADDRESS OF EMPLOYER	POSITION	EARNINGS	REASON FOR LEAVING

EDUCATION

	LOCATION	YEARS ATTENDED	DATE TO GRADUATE/GRADUATED
HIGH SCHOOL			
COLLEGE			

What are your hobbies, activities, interests and involvements? _____
_____

List achievements you feel are most meaningful. _____
_____

MEDICAL HISTORY

Are there any work activities for which you should not be considered or cannot perform because of a physical, mental, or medical disability? NO _____ YES _____ If yes, please explain _____
_____

Do you have any existing or recurring impairments (physical, mental, or medical) which require continuing or occasional treatment, special rest, diets, medicines, etc.? NO _____ YES _____ If yes, please explain _____

PERSONAL REFERENCES

NAME	ADDRESS	PHONE	RELATION	YRS. KNOWN

I affirm that the information provided on this application is true and complete to the best of my knowledge and agree that falsified information or significant omissions may disqualify me from further consideration for employment and may be considered justification for dismissal if discovered at a later date. Investigations and inquiries may be made of my personal, employment, financial, or medical history, and other related matters as may be necessary in arriving at a decision. I hereby release past employers, schools, and all persons contacted from all liability in responding to inquiries in connection with my application.

Date _____   _____
                                        APPLICANT OR EMPLOYEE SIGNATURE

THIS SECTION TO BE SIGNED BY EMPLOYEE ONLY AT TIME OF HIRE

I understand that it is Chick-fil-A's objective to provide the highest quality of food at competitive prices with the highest caliber of employees possible. In order to meet this objective, I acknowledge and consent as follows:

1. By submitting an application for employment with Chick-fil-A, I consent to having Chick-fil-A conduct an investigation regarding information contained in the application. I acknowledge, and consent to, that investigation, including contact with references and former employers, and an investigation regarding my credit and financial condition if relevant to the position for which I am applying. I also consent to any pre-hiring tests, including but not limited to paper and pencil honesty tests.

2. I acknowledge that Chick-fil-A may periodically conduct reasonable searches when I enter or leave the store premises. I expressly consent to this type of search and understand that by accepting employment at Chick-fil-A I am continuing my consent to search.

3. I acknowledge that Chick-fil-A may periodically conduct surveillance of the store premises or engage in other types of security procedures, including, but not limited to, paper and pencil honesty tests, the use of "marked" money in counter transactions or recording serial numbers of money used in counter transactions. I expressly consent to subject myself to surveillance and to these types of security procedures.

I understand that my consent to all of the security measures set forth is part of my application for employment with Chick-fil-A. I also understand that my continued consent to all these security measures set forth above is a pre-condition to my continued employment at Chick-fil-A, and that my failure to continue to consent to any of these measures may result in termination.

Date _____ _____

                                     Applicant or Employee Signature

APPLICANT SHOULD NOT WRITE BELOW THIS LINE

Comments of Interviewer:

Date: _____ Interviewer: _____

Chick-fil-A is an equal opportunity employer and considers all applicants equally without regard to race, sex, religion, national origin, color, handicap, citizenship, or veteran status.

THIS SECTION TO BE FILLED OUT BY INTERVIEWER ONLY AFTER HIRE

Date of Hire _____ Marital Status ____ M ____ S Number of Dependents _____
Rate of Pay _____ Male _____ Female _____ Date of Birth _____
Work Permit (If Minor)? _____ School Attending _____ Grade _____

_____
_____
_____
_____
_____
_____
_____
_____
_____
_____
_____

Chick-fil-A is an equal opportunity employer.   REVISED 7/88 personal finances later. The desire for "things" must be kept in check. Meeting the demands of today could seriously jeopardize plans for your future, such as college.

A part-time job is good training for both discipline and financial responsibility. If you have an income from a job, an allowance, or both, it is a good idea to sit down with parents or a good family friend and make out a simple budget that will match your needs. Please remember that every good and perfect gift comes from God, and He should be included in your budget.

" 'Bring all the tithes into the storehouse, that there may be food in My house, and try Me now in this,' says the LORD of hosts, 'If I will not open for you the windows of heaven and pour out for you such blessing that there will not be room enough to receive it' " (Malachi 3:5).

What an exciting promise!

Chapter 4

Challenges

1. As you see it, what are the basic, underlying principles of behavior as set forth in this chapter? Support your views with Scripture.

2. How will adherence to these acts of courtesy affect your future? Explain.

3. If the current attitude of youths toward the observance of the proper social behavior discussed in this chapter is that it is old-fashioned or out-of-date, how does a Christian young person handle it? Explain.

4. How can knowing and practicing correct social behavior help a young person develop maturity?

5. In your opinion, what circumstances govern the receiving of an allowance? Why?

6. What major responsibilities accompany a driver's license? Explain.

5

Dating

My son, do not forget my law, but let your heart keep my commands" (Proverbs 3:1). "For the commandment is a lamp, and the law is light; reproofs of instruction are the way of life" (Proverbs 6:23). "Keep my commands and live, and my law as the apple of your eye. Bind them on your fingers; write them on the tablet of your heart" (Proverbs 7:2–3).

It's natural for young men and women to have fellowship with one another. Your school and church provide plenty of opportunities to be together. We learn from one another and share interests. God ordained the sexes and planned that we should be companionable.

There comes a time, however, when you will be singled out by someone who wants to enjoy your company alone, away from the others—a "date," if you please. Occasional dates are part of the wholesome process of growing up. "Crowd dating" is fun, as you and your date join others in a crowd for some special function. Generally, dating begins around the age of sixteen. However, some may choose to wait until later. It's up to you *and your parents*.

Dating behavior is also Christian behavior, showing respect at all times. Holding hands and other gestures of fondness are never acceptable in public. Such actions are an indication of immaturity and are embarrassing to those around you.

"Going steady" isn't the best social arrangement for young people. Although it's flattering to know you are preferred above others, seeing only one person forces obligations. It restricts you from other friendships that add dimension to your life. It reduces your learning experiences in a period of your life when learning is important. You have a vast world ahead of you to explore, and it isn't wise to limit yourself by a demanding relationship. Try as you may, going steady can't be a casual relationship. The temptation to intimacy is apt to occur and other problems follow.

"My son, if sinners entice you, do not consent" (Proverbs 1:10). *"My son, hear the instruction of your father, and do not forsake the law of your mother"* (Proverbs 1:8).

Christians should date Christians. Young hearts are very susceptible, and you can avoid many problems down the road by following this rule. Every marriage began with a first date, and the Scripture is clear about unequally yoked marriages.

"Do not be unequally yoked together with unbelievers. For what fellowship has righteousness with lawlessness? And what communion has light with darkness? And what accord has Christ with Belial? Or what part has a believer with an unbeliever?" (2 Corinthians 6:14–16).

The dinner date

High-school graduation, if not some event before that, often brings a very special dating experience—the elegant restaurant. Here are a few tips to take the uneasiness out of it for you.

Make reservations. If you are delayed, call and advise the restaurant of your delay.

If you drive, a parking service may be provided, and an attendant will take your car when you arrive. He expects a tip

**The tapestry of life
is woven and made beautiful
with the magic threads
of being needed
by just one person.**

when you leave. (Tipping is covered in Appendix D.) If the weather is bad, the escort drives the young woman to the door, assists her out of the car, and then parks the car. She waits for him inside. If you are met by a doorman, allow him to help you out and open the door to the restaurant for you. A pleasant "thank you" is all he expects. If he calls a taxi for you when you leave, he will expect a tip.

Young men always check their coats if a checkroom is provided. Young women may take their coats to the table with them if they choose.

The maître d'hôtel (pronounced *"may-ter doe-tel"*) is the man who greets you. He is usually dressed in a dark suit or a tuxedo. The young man gives his name to the maître d'hôtel, who checks his reservation.

A captain or section headwaiter will direct you to a table. (In some restaurants you may be greeted by a hostess who greets and seats you.) As the young woman follows the headwaiter to the table, her escort follows her. The headwaiter generally pulls the chair out for her and may unfold a napkin and place it on her lap. It is acceptable to sit together on one side of a table (the wall side) or across from each other if you wish. The escort helps the young woman with her coat and arranges it on the back of the chair. If her handbag is large, it should go on the floor. She can keep a small one on her lap.

The headwaiter or hostess will hand menus to you, but the order is taken by a waitress or waiter, who serves you and receives your tip. A young woman should take her cue from her escort as to what to order. He might be able to make suggestions. She shouldn't order the most expensive or the least expensive item. The escort gives the order to the waiter. He may say, "My friend will have. . . ." If some of the words on the menu are unfamiliar, don't be intimidated. Ask the waiter. Giving information about the menu is part of his job.

To say no to wine at any time, place your fingers on the edge of the glass as the waiter approaches. It isn't necessary to turn the glass over or to place your palm over the glass.

Grace may be said silently with heads bowed or may be

given by the escort in low tones. Saying grace is proper and appropriate.

If there is a complaint for any reason, the escort should call the waiter. Be courteous, whether the problem is the food or some circumstance causing discomfort to you or your date.

Young women, a quick touch of makeup is permissible at the table, but anything more should be attended to in the powder room. If you must use the rest room during the meal, excuse yourself. Your date will understand. Some restaurants have attendants in the men's and women's rooms who expect tips for their services in providing a linen towel or just keeping the restroom clean. The tip is usually fifty cents to one dollar.

The waiter will bring the check on a small tray. Place the payment, usually cash or credit card, on the tray. The waiter will bring the change on the tray to the table. Leave the tip on the tray or include it on the credit card slip. The escort is the one to make the suggestion to leave.

With a group

In any group situation, be sure it is clearly understood who is paying for what. Paying the check can create problems that can destroy friendships. On a date, naturally the young man pays for his date. If you and your date are with a group (which often happens after gatherings such as church or games) in an informal setting and the waitress puts everything on one check and places it in front of you, it is all right to check the bill and pass it around for each to see what his part is. However, at a dinner in a restaurant, prior to ordering you will be asked about how the checks should be made—all on one or separate. In the event that everything is mistakenly put on one bill, pay it. Surely the others will reimburse you. If they don't, you don't need friends like that. Be prepared for such a situation. It may arise!

Tipping is required, and the usual amount is 15 percent

of the bill. If the meal is paid for with a credit card, you may write the amount of the tip in the space provided on the credit slip when signing.

Sports events

Most Americans have some interest in one or several sports. Professional games are generally so well attended that it is difficult to get good seats without reservations made long in advance or a season ticket.

There are not too many rules for social behavior at such events except courtesy and consideration for others around you. That means no shouting of insults to the opposing team or jumping up and down blocking the views of those around you.

If invited to a game with which you are not familiar, learn something about the game before you attend. Learn the basic rules and what to watch for. Act interested, even if you are bored. Your actions might come through as disinterested or disloyal.

Large crowds require special considerations. You may get lost from your friends, and so it is advisable to have a meeting place preplanned. Also, whether with an escort or friends, remember where the car is parked (make a mental note of aisles or lanes). Don't push or shove at the slightest provocation when you are in a line—a crowd can get out of control.

For young women only

When you are asked for a date, respond with pleasure. Even if you would rather not accept, make an effort to spare his feelings. Some young men have an unreasonable fear of rejection. You don't have to accept. Tell him that you appreciate the invitation, but you'll have to check with your parents. Ask him when you can get back to him with an answer. In any event, find out the time, place, and the type of clothing to wear. You wouldn't wear your Sunday best to a hayride, for instance. A young woman shouldn't accept a date from someone she knows only casually. It's important to know something of his background and character.

If he calls by phone, he might be shy and need a little help. You can help eliminate the awkwardness by being friendly and relaxed. Make a casual remark or bring up a subject of mutual interest. Ask a question. This always helps the conversation to flow.

He may wait for you to end the call. He may not be aware that the caller ends the call. Simply say, "John, I'm sorry, but I really have to say good-bye now." You may give a reason if you have one or can think of a good, honest one.

Always be forthright and up-front in your relationships, keeping in mind, however, that young men have feelings, too! Be sure your plans meet with the approval of your parents.

If you must decline a date regretfully, you can decline by saying, "No, I can't make it this time [you might tell him the reason], but please ask me again."

Always be forthright and up-front in your relationships.

In certain situations you may need to phone a young man. Make the call brief. Save the chitchat for when he calls you—that is, if he is interested in your chitchat and if he isn't calling long-distance.

If you have to change your plans, let your date know. Or if you have to be late, call. It's always considerate to advise another person of any change of plans where he is involved.

When it's time for the date, have him come to your home. It's in poor taste to meet him somewhere. Allow him to come to your home, ring the doorbell, and ask for you. Be ready! Introduce him to your parents, and be sure there is a clear understanding of when he should bring you home. You may ask him to have a seat, but it will be up to you to make the suggestion to leave.

If you are a licensed driver and he is not, and you have the use of the family car, allow him to bring you home if at all possible. It is better not to drop him off at his home and drive home alone. Prior arrangements could be made with your family to see him to his home. This may not be an ideal arrangement, but it is a reasonable solution to the problem of an unlicensed escort. Allow him to be courteous by opening doors (car doors, too), holding your coat, or carrying objects. Be natural and relaxed.

In a group, you may be tempted to talk with girlfriends, but don't wander away from your date or get into long conversations with others. Be attentive. On the other hand, allow your date some conversational time with others. Clinging or being possessive is uncomfortable for everyone.

When you enter an auditorium, follow the usher and enter the row of seats first. If it is a double date, the two young women sit together with a young man on either side.

Whatever the occasion of the date, it is your responsibility to be cheerful. Compliment the food (even if it's a hamburger), the program or event, and his thoughtfulness. He will be much more apt to invite you again if you tell him how enjoyable the time together has been.

If he has forgotten the hour you are to be home, remind him. It is usually your responsibility to suggest leaving a gathering. If you are going to be late, by all means telephone your parents.

When you return home, you may invite him in if your parents are home. If he stays too long, give him a gentle hint. As for a good-night kiss—NO. No young man should expect a kiss. This may be a pattern of some, but you are a Christian young woman dating a Christian young man. Kisses are the language of true love, the beginning of intimacy, and they must be saved for that permanent, lasting relationship. You must exercise your character strength. He will respect you for it.

For young men only

When you ask a young woman for a date, be sure you've made all the necessary arrangements. Speak to her either in person or by phone. How you ask is important. It isn't a good idea to ask, "What are you doing Saturday evening?" That forces her to tell you her plans. If she has no plans, she has to accept your invitation or admit to not being interested in going with you. Spare her and yourself from that awkward situation. State your plans, and simply invite her to be your guest. Give her time to consider by telling her she can give you an answer later. Plan to either see her again or call her for her answer. Give her an opportunity to discuss the date with her parents.

If you call her by phone, be sensitive to her interest in talking with you. If she wants to chitchat, it will be obvious to you. The caller always ends the call. Avoid last-minute calling for dates because she might think that she isn't your first choice.

If you have to change your plans, let your date know. Or if you have to be late, call. It's always considerate to advise another person of any change of plans where she is involved.

Flowers are appropriate for more formal occasions and are a nice touch on almost any occasion. When you plan to send flowers, consult your date in advance on the color of the dress she will be wearing.

Go to your date's home to call for her. There may be a few situations (but very few) where it is acceptable to meet her elsewhere. Ring the doorbell and be gracious when introduced to her parents. Be sure that you understand and observe her curfew time. That time is generally established by her parents.

If she is a licensed driver and you are not, and she has the use of her family car, don't allow her to drop you off and drive home alone. Go home with her and have your way home arranged previously.

Be courteous at all times. Practice all the good manners you have learned. (We hope they are natural to you.) Open doors (including the car), help her with her wraps, and carry packages if necessary. Be natural and relaxed.

In a group, don't wander away from your date or get into long conversations with others. Be attentive. On the other hand, allow her some conversational time. Clinging or being possessive is uncomfortable for everyone.

If you attend a function held in an auditorium, allow her to follow the usher and enter the row of seats. You follow and sit beside her. If she needs her wrap around her shoulders, assist her. Remember to be attentive and polite, the answer to nearly every social situation.

If you aren't sure of what to talk about, plan a little in advance. Think of some subjects of mutual interest. You'll be surprised how smoothly the conversation will go. Have a good sense of humor. A bit of laughter lightens the heart!

When you return to her home, she may invite you in. Accept only if her parents are at home. Avoid any lingering good-nights in a parked car. This is disrespectful to parents and too often a source for neighborhood gossip. Remember to be friendly, not too talkative, and make your stay short. As for a kiss—NO! This may be the pattern for some worldly young people, but remember your Christian principles. Kissing is the language of true love. It is the first step toward intimacy and must be saved for the lasting relationship that God may have planned for you down the road. Many Christian guidance counselors advise against any physical contact at all, which includes holding hands. Physical contact leads to emotional entanglements. A word to the wise—beware!

Chapter 5

Challenges

1. Why is "going steady" not the best social arrangement for young people? Explain.

2. Why is it important for Christians to date Christians?

3. In group dining, how can you avoid problems associated with paying the check?

4. How can a young woman graciously refuse a date? Give some examples.

5. In your opinion, why is it in poor taste for a young woman to meet a young man for a date somewhere other than at her home?

6. How is character strength shown in the dating experience? Explain.

7. What advice can you give to young people for pleasant and worthwhile dating?

8. Young men, what qualities do you look for in the young women you select to date? Young women, what qualities do you look for in a young man before you accept a date?

9. How important is parental advice in the dating process? Explain.

10. Where does "do not be unequally yoked" (2 Corinthians 6:14) fit into dating?

6

Friends and Friendship

A true friend is priceless and should be treated with great care. A little saying goes, "A friend is someone who knows all about you and loves you anyway." A friend provides support, comfort, and understanding.

What is a friend?

"A friend loves at all times" (Proverbs 17:17).
If a friend *loves* at all times, what is love? The Bible says,

> *Love suffers long and is kind; love does not envy; love does not parade itself, is not puffed up; does not behave rudely, does not seek its own, is not provoked, thinks no evil; does not rejoice in iniquity, but rejoices in the truth. . . . Love never fails* (1 Corinthians 13:4–8).

Being a friend is quite a role to fulfill.

Friends also provide constructive criticism and, when it is given, accept it and act on it. Many personality faults can be corrected if the sincere correction received from a friend is heeded. Keep in mind that family members can be friends, too. We often forget that our parents fill many different roles in our lives, including the role of friend.

Some young people seem to make friends easily. Others find it more difficult. We are all familiar with the "popular"

type, everyone's friend. However, with a closer look, do
these people fit the above description of a friend? Perhaps
that explains why some of these friendships aren't lasting.
The qualities that go into making true friendship aren't
always up-front or on display.

There are many ingredients that go into making and developing friendship. To have friends, you must be friendly
(Proverbs 18:24). Be honest in your communication. Many
young people conceal their emotions because they aren't sure
they can share them or they feel they won't be understood. A
good friend can be trusted and is able to enter into another's
spirit and appreciate his/her deepest feelings. Don't rush into
close friendships; they take time to develop.

Hindrances to friendship

It's interesting to listen to the complaints young people
have about one another. Borrowing is high on the complaint
list of young women. Sharing is an act of graciousness, but
borrowing is taking advantage of a friend. When you ask to
borrow something from a friend, the friend may not want to
lend it to you, but will oblige for fear of losing your friendship. This destroys the foundation of good friendship. It's
best not to borrow at all except in an extreme emergency (Romans 13:8).

Don't rush into close friendships;
they take time to develop.

Conceit or snobbishness also ranks high on the list of
complaints. You may not be aware of this problem. It isn't
only a matter of what you think or feel about yourself; it can
also be what others perceive you to be. Unfortunately, we
can't see ourselves as others see us. A good friend can help
you in this area. To be conceited or snobbish runs counter to
Christlikeness and is a colossal block in making friends.

A friend is
someone to whom one can pour out
all the contents of one's heart,
chaff and grain together,
knowing that the gentlest of hands
will take and sift it,
keep what is worth keeping,
and with the breath of kindness
blow the rest away.

—Arabian proverb

Jealousy, when used in the Bible in reference to God, means "requiring complete loyalty and faithfulness." When used elsewhere, it is usually in reference to a relationship with a person. It means "grudging," "resentful," or "envious." Without a doubt one of the most devastating of all human traits, jealousy destroys friendships.

"Envy is rottenness to the bones" (Proverbs 14:30).

Wars have been fought, murders committed, and homes and families destroyed because of this rottenness within. Cain killed his brother Abel (Genesis 4:8), Jacob stole his brother's birthright (Genesis 25:33), and Joseph's brothers sold him into slavery (Genesis 37:28), all because of jealousy. God, in His wisdom, gave a very powerful commandment to Moses, included in the ten handed down on Mount Sinai (Exodus 20:17).

How sad that so little attention is given to getting rid of this deadly sin. Jealousy begins in early childhood among brothers and sisters, then extends to peers in the school years, and continues in one form or another as people go on into marriage and a career. But there is no place in the Christian's heart for this evil trait. God made provision for the removal of jealousy along with all other sins through the death and resurrection of Christ and the daily cleansing by the Holy Spirit.

A word of caution: be alert to this sin of jealousy. It can enter so easily and can grow into devastating proportions, causing irreparable damage before you realize it. Say with the psalmist in Psalm 19:12, *"Cleanse me from secret faults."*

Many people have little mannerisms or personal habits that hinder friendship. Take a good, close look at yourself as you go through this checklist. Do you

- Make annoying facial expressions?
- Chew or "pop" gum?
- Bite your fingernails?
- Poke or nudge?
- Sniffle (without a handkerchief)?
- Giggle?

- Make silly noises?
- Talk loudly and interrupt others?
- Pick your nose?
- Grind your teeth?

These are just a few of the things people usually won't tell you—unless, of course, it's a friend with whom you have established a great deal of understanding.

Making and keeping friends

It's difficult to pinpoint what the "something" is that makes some people so attractive and popular. It isn't always good looks. It's a composite of many things, to be sure, with the fruit of the Spirit at the top of the list. (See Galatians 5:22–26.) Some people take courses in charm, success, and similar topics. These courses are geared to making them likable, believable, and therefore successful in whatever they attempt to do. Heed the following Biblical suggestions, and you will be a friend blessed with an abundance of friends. You will also be an effective representative for Christ.

- Honor God; respect authority. (This includes parents!)
- Be sincere, friendly, and natural.
- Be modest, not jealous or boastful. (Boasting is a subtle way of putting others down.)
- Be considerate of others; be unselfish.
- Keep aggressiveness in check.
- Be loyal and honest; don't gossip.
- Include those around you in your conversation.
- Be clean and well-groomed.
- Use good table manners.
- Borrow only in an emergency, and return the item promptly.
- Keep good company. You are known by the company you keep.
- Avoid being possessive of friends.
- Maintain a good disposition without a display of temper or ill will. Don't argue with others.

- Be a good loser.
- Be quick to offer assistance where needed.
- Be fair.
- Be quick to apologize or admit a mistake.
- Live by your own principles, maintaining your own convictions that are in line with biblical ones.

Gifts and giving

Gifts are expressions of how you feel. They can say to friends and acquaintances, "Thank you," "I love you," "I'm sorry," "Get well," "Come again," "Have a good time," "I wish you happiness," or "Congratulations." A gift doesn't have to be expensive, but it should be appropriate, contain a gift card or enclosure, and be wrapped tastefully.

Gifts can be given without an occasion, but they are usually expected for the following events: "Bon Voyages" (farewells), the awarding of doctorates, graduations of any kind, weddings, bridal showers, baby showers, hospital stays, and birthdays.

A gift to your hostess is also expected following a stay of several days or more. You may present it as you leave or shortly thereafter. However, it doesn't replace the "bread-and-butter" (thank-you) letter that you should send after a visit.

Common courtesies to consider

According to the *Thorndike-Barnhart Dictionary, courtesy* means "being polite and thoughtful of others." Here are some specific ways to show courtesy to friends, acquaintances, and strangers, in a variety of situations:

1. Be sincere with compliments.
2. Accept compliments with a "thank you." Rejecting a compliment in any way shows a lack of poise.

3. Avoid asking personal questions.
4. Don't congratulate a bride—wish her happiness and give the congratulations to the groom.
5. Look mildly inattentive if an off-color joke is told in your presence. Don't encourage such talk by attention of any kind. Avoid comment.
6. Say "please" when asking for a favor.
7. Say "excuse me" when leaving the presence of someone.
8. Use "pardon me" or "I'm sorry" when you bump into someone, spill something on someone, break something, interrupt a conversation, or want to correct something you've already said.
9. Don't cut into lines, no matter what "good" reason you think you have or what "important person" you may be accompanying.
10. Be fair with "air time" when talking, either in person or on the phone.
11. Don't give orders. Make requests by saying, "Would you please . . . ?"
12. Listen when someone is talking.
13. Don't use a toothpick or pick at your teeth in front of anyone. The same rule applies to blowing your nose and to clipping and manicuring your nails.
14. Don't stare or point at anyone.
15. Don't eat while walking.
16. Avoid yawning in the presence of other people.
17. Cover your nose and mouth when sneezing or coughing.
18. Don't occupy the most comfortable seat if older persons are present.
19. Don't interrupt a conversation. If an interruption is urgent, use an "I'm sorry, but . . ."

Trying to remember all these guidelines will be very difficult if they are new to you. Practice them as often as possible and gradually they will become a part of the new, courteous you who is considerate of others at all times.

Persons with disabilities

Persons with physical or mental disabilities are *persons*—with strengths, capabilities, desires, ambitions, values, beliefs. Treat them with the same respect you accord anyone else. Here are a few do's and don'ts to help you avoid some common blunders:

Do talk directly to her ("Would you care for some tea?" "Are you enjoying the party?" "How do you like school this year?").

Don't use the third person to ask someone else about her ("Would she like some tea?" "Is she enjoying the party?" "How does she like school this year?").

Do talk in a normal tone of voice.

Don't raise your voice when talking to a person who is blind. (He's blind, not deaf.)

Do enunciate clearly when talking to a person who is hearing impaired.

Don't turn your head or put your hand over your mouth when talking to a person who watches your lip movements to aid his comprehension.

Do offer your arm to a person who is blind (guide her hand to the crook of your arm).

Don't grab her arm and attempt to steer.

Do offer to carry refreshments for a person on crutches or in a wheelchair.

Don't be overly solicitous. If he says he can handle it, take him at his word.

Do ask how you can help if she has an accident or falls.

Don't treat her like a newborn who got bopped on the soft spot. She's probably more embarrassed than hurt and would appreciate as little fuss as possible.

Do ask a person with a speech difficulty to repeat himself if you don't catch what he says. Say, "I'm sorry, I didn't understand. Could you say it again?"

Don't pretend you understand when you don't. To do so implies that what he says doesn't really matter.

Do be relaxed and sincere. Talk about anything you'd talk to anyone else about.

Don't affect a pasted-on cheerfulness and talk "down" as if to a child.

Do include the person with a disability in your conversation or activity.

Don't assume that she can't or doesn't want to participate—ask her.

Most persons with disabilities prefer no special treatment, and as you can see, most of the preceding do's and don'ts are commonsense courtesies. You can't go wrong if you ask yourself, "How would *I* like to be treated?"

Giving a party

Parties are fun! They provide opportunities to make new friends and get to know old friends better. Also, parties help young people develop poise, confidence, and self-esteem.

A good party takes planning ahead. Start first with parental approval. Let them help you decide where the party will be and how many guests to invite. If the party is to be indoors, at your home, you will limit your guests according to the space available. Outdoor parties are very popular, perhaps because they eliminate the tension of spilled beverages and any damage to furnishings. Include your parents and have them or an adult chaperone on hand for any emergencies that might arise and provide transportation for guests. Mother is a great help in the kitchen, and Dad is an expert with those folding chairs and tables. However, it's your party, and you should do most of the work.

After you have decided on a place, consider the time. Invitations should go out, by mail or phone, at least two weeks in advance. Card shops have a good assortment of party invitations, or you can make your own. They should include the date, the time and place, the type of party (Valentine, birthday, graduation), the name of the host or hostess, and any special instructions such as what to wear or bring. Be sure to state if you will provide transportation.

To avoid hurt feelings, be selective when you are preparing your guest list. Invite only those persons who have some special tie to you or to the occasion for the party. For example, if it is a going-away party for Mary, invite Mary's friends. There is no simple way to avoid hurt feelings. If there are unintentional oversights, it is best to go to the persons directly and express regrets. Be open, up-front, and honest. They will appreciate your honesty.

Choose a time (weekends or holidays) when guests aren't obligated to do homework or study for tests. Plan transportation and provide it for guests if needed, especially after the party.

Food should be simple and inexpensive. Don't try to outdo your friends with party fare. Most young people seem to be happy with the usual—pizza, hamburgers, hot dogs, chips, and beverages. When food is served, remember to say grace. Include Christ in all your planning.

Plan games that all guests can participate in. Be sensitive to guests who are shy, and don't plan games that require a display of wit. This puts some guests at a disadvantage, particularly if the game is new to them. Keep guests together, and do not provide an opportunity for some to wander off in pairs.

If you have included the hours on the invitations, guests

will know when they must leave. Allow friends to help with the cleanup. Then be sure to show your gratitude to your parents by putting things in order after the guests have departed.

As a host or hostess, be alert to the needs of your guests and your parties will always be a success. Maintain your Christian dignity, whether attending or giving a party, by showing respect to parents, furnishings and, of course, the guests.

Invitations

For an informal party at your home, if you choose, you may phone the invitations instead of mailing written ones. Be sure to give the what, when, and where. If the party is honoring someone's birthday, gifts should be given unless the invitation, whether written or phoned, indicates otherwise. It is important for the person invited to reply promptly, within a day or two.

R.S.V.P.

If you receive an invitation with an R.S.V.P. on it, it means that you must reply very promptly. If the R.S.V.P. is followed by a telephone number, you are expected to phone your reply. If the invitation says, "regrets only," your presence will be expected unless you phone or write your regrets.

Chapter 6

Challenges

1. What is a friend? Support your views with Scripture references.

2. List at least five hindrances to friendship.

3. In your opinion, what are the most common complaints young people have about one another?

4. What is jealousy? How does it affect friendship?

5. List some basic reasons (not occasions) for giving gifts.

6. When and why do you respond or not respond to an invitation?

7

Introductions and Greetings

Introductions are opportunities for lasting impressions. Knowing a few simple rules can help you make the most of getting acquainted.

General rules

The three basic rules are

1. A man is always introduced to a woman. (The only exception to this rule is in family introductions.)

   EXAMPLE: *Jane, this is my college friend, Andy Jones. Andy, this is Jane Smith.*

2. A younger person is introduced to an older person.

   EXAMPLE: *Uncle Henry, this is my tennis partner, Bob Wills.*

3. A person who holds a position of lesser importance (by title or distinction) is introduced to a person who holds a position of greater importance.

   EXAMPLE: *Senator Stofford, my sister, Miss Smith.*

Note: Except for members of your own family, a woman is never presented to a man unless he is (a) the head of a country or President of the United States, (b) a member of a royal family, (c) a church official, or (d) an older man in a high position.

EXAMPLE: *Bishop Stevens, I'd like you to meet my violin instructor, Karen Avery.*

When you are introduced to someone, respond with "Hello" or "How do you do?" or "How are you?" Avoid affected replies, such as "Charmed" or "Delighted." If you should say more, say what is appropriate: "It's nice to meet you," or "I've been looking forward to meeting you." Always stand when you are introduced to a woman or to an elderly man. Also, it's a good idea to repeat the person's name.

EXAMPLE: *I'm happy to meet you, Mr. Jones.*

It's a great help in remembering names. There may be times when you can't recall a name. If that happens, it's proper to ask.

EXAMPLE: *I'm sorry, I'll have to ask your name.*

If you sense that someone you've met very recently has forgotten your name, be helpful and give a clue in your conversation. It isn't polite to ask someone you met some time ago if he remembers you. If you feel he doesn't recognize you, introduce yourself, and your conversation may bring back a memory of having met you previously.

As for introducing stepparents or stepbrothers and stepsisters, you may refer to them as *stepmother/stepfather, stepbrother, stepsister,* or you may simply say *mother/father, brother, sister.* The choice is up to you. Either is correct. In family introductions, it is courteous and correct to mention the name of the other person first.

EXAMPLE: *Mr. Jones, I'd like you to meet my mother, Sarah Livingston.*

Speak gently! 'Tis a little thing
Dropped in the heart's deep well;
The good, the joy that it may bring
Eternity shall tell.

—G. W. Langford

To introduce in-laws, avoid the use of the term *in-law* and introduce them as your spouse's parents.

> EXAMPLE: *Mrs. Jones, I'd like you to meet my husband's parents, Mr. and Mrs. Smith.*

It is a violation of good manners to call parents by their first names. This undermines respect and appears you are trying to establish a sibling relationship rather than the natural parent-child relationship. An attitude that accepts and respects an age difference is much better. If your spouse's parents prefer for you to call them by their first names, that is a different matter and should be handled according to their wishes.

If you are in a group where most people know one another and are on a first-name basis, you may say, "Alice Jones, John Smith" or "Alice, this is John Smith—Alice Jones." Be careful not to say, "my friend," which implies that the other person is not a friend. If you don't know the first names of both, be consistent and use a title—Miss, Mrs., or Mr.—for each person.

Some titles are used only for introduction while another title is used for the same person when you are speaking to him/her. A Protestant minister who has a doctorate should be introduced as "The Reverend Doctor Jones," but he should be spoken to as "Doctor Jones." If he doesn't have a doctorate, "The Reverend John Jones" is his introductory title, and you would speak to him as "Mister Jones." A Catholic priest is introduced as "Father" and addressed the same way. A Jewish rabbi is introduced and addressed as "Rabbi Stein" or, if he has a doctorate, as "Doctor Stein." Medical doctors and dentists are called "Doctor Jones" both in introductions and in conversation. College professors are referred to as "Professor Jones" or "Doctor Jones" if he or she has a doctorate. A senator is introduced as "Senator Smith" but addressed as "Senator," "Madam," or "Sir," while a member of the House of Representatives is introduced as "Representative Smith" and addressed as "Mister Smith." A nun is introduced and addressed as "Sister Margaret."

First name usage

To call an older person, particularly one of distinction, by his or her first name reflects an attitude of disrespect. There are some special incidents where first names are requested, thus making their use appropriate, but those incidents are rare.

When an older person calls a younger person by his or her first name, that is not to be interpreted as an invitation to respond in the same manner. There are some definite rules about *not* using first names. Do not use first names with a business client, a customer, a person of higher position or rank (senator, governor, teacher), a professional person (doctor, lawyer, minister), or a superior in a business office.

On the street

If you're walking down the street with a friend and you encounter a second friend, introductions aren't necessary if it is a brief meeting. Friend number one may walk ahead or stand to one side. If it appears that the conversation may be fairly long, friend number one should be introduced to friend number two. All of you should step to the side of the walk, out of the traffic pattern.

In the home

When you are invited into a home, your host or hostess will meet you at the door and assist you with your wraps before introducing you to other family members or guests. Be friendly and gracious. Don't take a seat until invited to do so. If introductions take place around a table, handshakes are in order if it does not mean moving from your assigned place or stretching across the table.

When you make a social call in a home, remain standing until invited to sit down. If the hostess wasn't present at your arrival, rise when she enters the room. Shake hands only if she extends her hand.

When you are ready to leave, if there is a large group present, don't tour the room telling everyone good-bye. Say good-bye to those nearest you, thank your host and hostess, and depart.

When acquaintances come to your home, open the door graciously, greet them with a warm greeting, and invite them in. Ask if you may take their wraps, and as you indicate a chair, you should say, "Will you please sit down?"

When guests linger too long, tell them you have a big day tomorrow (or whatever is appropriate but true) and that you have to call it a day. Be honest and direct. If they are friends, they surely will understand.

Shaking hands

Men always shake hands on meeting. Handshakes between men and women are always initiated by women. Young women usually don't shake hands with other young people, but shaking hands with older people (when they initiate it) is a sign of respect. Always shake hands with anyone who offers a hand. It's an insult to ignore such a greeting. A handshake should be a firm, friendly clasp without shaking or pumping. If someone will just not let go, a gentle pulling away is in order.

Standing or sitting

It's correct for a woman to remain seated when she is introduced. However, she stands to meet an elderly person or a distinguished person. Men stand whenever a woman (of any age) enters the room and remain standing until she is seated.

Group introductions

Group introductions are fairly simple. Mention the name of the new person first, then give the names of the others in the order they are arranged in the room. If you aren't sure of all the names, suggest they introduce themselves. As a conversation starter, you may say, "Jody is visiting from Schroon Lake, New York." If it's a very large group, introduce the new-

---

A handshake should be a firm, friendly clasp without shaking or pumping.

---

comer to a circle of guests. It may be impossible to introduce everyone. However, everyone should be introduced to the guest of honor if there is one. If you are a guest and the hostess overlooks you, don't leave without meeting the one for whom the party is given. Introduce yourself. You may say, "I'm Carolyn Smith, a friend of Jill's [the hostess]."

A receiving line

If you attend any function where there is a receiving line, your hostess or the first person in the line will present you to the guest of honor on her right, who will present you to the person on her right, and so on. Shake hands and say, "How do you do?" Try not to hold up the line by chatting. If you don't know the person at the head of the line, introduce yourself. A young man should introduce himself first and then the young woman who is with him. Embraces aren't appropriate in a formal receiving line for heads of state and government officials. Wedding receiving lines are considered formal but to a lesser degree. Guests are often close friends or family from distant places, and a kiss or embrace may be expected.

Chapter 7

Challenges

1. Why are correct introductions important?

2. How do you correctly handle forgetting a name when introducing someone?

3. How do you introduce
    - A Protestant minister?
    - A Catholic priest?
    - A Jewish rabbi?
    - A medical doctor?
    - A senator?
    - A member of the House of Representatives?

4. What are the general rules for group introductions?

5. When is it appropriate to call a person by his/her first name? When is it not appropriate?

Sharing Our Daily Bread

*N**ow it came to pass, as He sat at the table with them, that He took bread, blessed and broke it, and gave it to them* (Luke 24:30).

Eating, especially with friends, is a very pleasant experience. However, not knowing how to handle the utensils or not being sure how to handle new foods can be awkward if not embarrassing. Many young people say they do not enjoy a dinner date because they are so self-conscious about eating that they can never relax. So, knowing the rules and practicing them will make it easier for you. A person's good breeding shows up clearly in table manners, and it only makes good sense to spend a little extra time learning how to eat with poise. Here are some guidelines that will help, whether you are dining in a home, a restaurant, or a banquet hall.

Dinner is served

Adjust your chair to a comfortable distance from the table as you sit down.

If a young man is seated to the left of a young woman, he should pull out her chair for her and push it under her gently as she sits down. If he is the only man at the table, he should also seat another woman. Of course, he wouldn't be expected to go around the table (assuming he is the only man

present) and seat all the women. Some discretion has to be
used.

Sit erect and keep your elbows to your sides. Elbows
may rest on the table between courses, but never while you
are eating.

When the host or hostess indicates who will say grace,
bow your head until the "amen" has been said.

How to begin

Watch your host or hostess as he/she picks up the napkin. That is your signal to pick up yours. Place your napkin,
folded in half, on your lap, with the open edges toward you if
it is large (dinner size). Open smaller napkins (luncheon size)
entirely. After the meal, casually fold the napkin and place it
to the left side of the plate. If a napkin ring is used, remove
the napkin and place the ring to the upper left side of the
plate. When you are finished, refold the napkin, put it into
the ring, and place it to the left of your plate. Treat paper
napkins the same as cloth ones.

If some flatware is missing at your plate and the host or
hostess doesn't notice, ask for what you need. Don't use your
own spoon if a serving spoon has been forgotten. Ask for the
needed piece.

Declining wine

An occasion may arise where you will be invited to a
dinner where wine is served. The glasses will be on the table.
It is correct, as the wine is served, to gently touch your glass
and say "No, thank you." There are many teetotalers in our
society. This need not be embarrassing to anyone. If the wine
is already on the table, just don't drink it. It's that simple.

The Full Circle of Life

To share is to live,
To live is to love,
To love is to care,
To care is to *share*.

Toasting an honored guest

Should the host or hostess propose a toast, don't be per-plexed. A *toast* simply means, "Here's to love, friendship, health, wealth, and happiness." The custom of toasting goes back into history, and it is merely a gesture of raising a glass toward the person of honor in unison with the other guests at the motion of the host or hostess. The person being toasted does not raise his or her glass. If wine is served some will, of course, toast with wine. Many times Christians who do not drink wine are in such situations, but there is always an ap-propriate response. It is correct to raise an empty glass or a glass of water.

You are served

The guest of honor is served first, and then the serving continues counterclockwise around the table. The hostess serves herself last and her husband next to last.

Wait for your hostess to begin eating. At a large gather-ing, however, she may insist that you begin while the food is hot. If food is served by a servant, the food is served from the left. The plate is removed from the right. The food is served to the first woman on the right of the host, then proceeds around the table. If food is served family style, receive it with the right hand and pass it with the left.

Wait for your hostess to begin eating.

The hostess always serves the dessert, even though the host may have served the main course. It's a good idea to serve the dessert directly from the table since that saves a lot of steps.

In some homes the host may serve from a stack of plates in front of him. He serves the main dish, and he may also choose to serve the vegetables. The vegetable dishes may be passed around if preferred.

The first plate is given to the woman on his right (the guest of honor), and the next plate is passed down to the end of the table to the person seated there (generally the hostess). The rest of the guests on the right are served in order, working back to the head of the table. The process is repeated for the guests on the left.

Because this process takes time, grace is usually said before any serving begins. The host will suggest the guests begin eating after three or four persons have been served.

If a salad is served, it is usually on the table in separate salad dishes or the salad bowl is passed around.

The dessert may be on separate plates (waiting in the kitchen) to be served when the table has been cleared or the hostess (or person at the opposite end of the table) may serve it in the same way the host served the main course.

Use of table flatware

There are two accepted ways for using flatware (silverware): the American way, which means shifting the fork from hand to hand, and the European way, which means holding the fork in the left hand most of the time.

For the American way, hold the knife by the handle in the right hand, with the forefinger pointed toward the blade. Hold the fork (with the prongs down) in the left hand in a similar way. Never hold any utensil in a fist. Place the fork in the food to be cut and cut only *one piece at a time*. Lay the knife on the plate and change the fork to the right hand. Hold the fork as you hold a pencil, lifting the food to your mouth with the prongs up.

It's permissible to use a small piece of bread as a pusher for bits of food (such as peas), but if you want the last taste of the gravy, use your fork (rather than your hand) with a small piece of bread. Don't use bread as a gravy or sauce sopper.

Lay your knife and fork (prongs up) when not in use across the upper right "corner" of the plate. Place flatware in this same position when you finish eating. To "gangplank" your utensils (one end on the plate and the other on the table) is not acceptable.

Don't hold a knife or fork in your hand while drinking from a glass. It's acceptable to hold a piece of flatware in your hand while talking, but don't wave it around to make a point.

Yes, you may use a knife to cut your salad. The salad knife and fork are used in the same way as the dinner knife and fork. Leave the knife and fork on the salad plate when you have finished, or the fork in the individual salad bowl.

When you are eating soup, use the soup spoon. If there is no soup spoon, use the spoon provided, and always spoon *away* from you. If thin soup is served in a cup with a handle, you may drink it directly from the cup. You may put small crackers into soup, but don't crumble crackers into it. Leave your spoon on the soup plate, not in the bowl or cup.

This placement of used flatware applies to desserts as well. *Never* place used flatware on the tablecloth.

An iced-tea spoon with a long handle is always a problem. After you've used it, place it on the service plate; however, if there is no service plate, you have no choice but to drink your tea without stirring. You can't place a wet spoon on the tablecloth.

The European way of using flatware differs from the American way on several points. After you cut food, instead of shifting the fork to the right hand to eat, keep it in the left hand, and carry the food to the mouth with the prongs of the fork down. You may use the knife as a pusher to put small pieces of food onto the fork. If you use a fork without a knife, you should hold it in the right hand with the prongs up, American fashion. When it's not in use, rest the knife on the right side of the plate, pointing to the upper left, with the sharp edge of the blade toward the center of the plate and the handle slightly over the edge of the plate. To *rest* the fork, place it, prongs down, pointing from lower left to upper right of the plate, with handle slightly over the edge of the plate. When you have finished, place the knife in the rest position and the fork, prongs down, parallel to it on the side toward you.

The dessert flatware is put down on the plate when you are finished. If a low and shallow bowl is used for dessert, you may leave the spoon in it, or on the plate below. If a fork is used, place the fork prongs down from lower right to upper left.

All doubts about using flatware can be removed if you remember to work from the outside in. You can always follow the lead of your hostess. Don't worry about mistakes. Everyone makes them!

A buffet

A buffet dinner is probably one of the best and most practical ways to serve a large group. Guests seem to enjoy a buffet dinner. They are more relaxed and may take only the foods they like—and young people have decided tastes!

If the buffet dinner is in the home, the food is usually placed on the dining table. Guests file around the table counterclockwise, picking up napkins, plates, utensils, and food.

Each person helps himself, but it is correct for a man to help a woman by filling her plate and taking it to her while she remains seated. Also, if halfway through the meal a man sees a woman with an empty plate, he may ask, "May I get something for you?"

If there is a problem with buffet dinners, it is with the seating. Small tables are ideal. They can be set attractively and place cards may be used. If you are expected to sit in the living room with your plate in your lap, your beverage can be a problem. You may put your glass or cup on your plate, or you may place it on a table near you—but only if a coaster or mat is available. Never put a cup, saucer, glass, or plate on unprotected furniture.

It is awkward and inconvenient to attempt to maneuver to a seat with both a beverage and a plate. If you are to be seated at a table, you may prefer to take your plate first and return for your beverage. If you will not be seated at a table, it is best to place the beverage on your plate as you move to your seat. If beverages are not set out, your host or hostess will serve your beverage where you are seated.

If the buffet is in a place outside the home, the table is usually positioned in the center of the room. Guests file around the table, as in the home. In very large gatherings, seating may be limited or unavailable. If this is the case, place your beverage cup or glass on your plate. Do not linger at the food table or carry on a conversation there. Go back to the food table as many times as you wish, but take small portions.

When you are finished eating, carry your used plates to a place designated. Do not put them on the food table! If there is a dessert table, follow the procedure as for the main course. Dessert plates and utensils will be provided for you.

It's an insult to the cook
to shake salt or pepper
over food you haven't tasted.

A good host or hostess will make things very simple for you. The idea is to relax and enjoy your friends and the food. This is a good time to meet new people. If you are seated next to a stranger, be quick to introduce yourself and your guest or companion. Be friendly, use lots of smiles, and there will be many more dinners ahead for you!

Eating with poise

Remember these general rules for eating with poise:
Take small mouthfuls.

Don't talk with your mouth full, but practice talking with a small amount of food, should you have to answer someone.

If you encounter something you can't chew, put it on your fork, and holding it closely to your mouth, place it on your plate from the fork. If it's a fruit pit, place it from your mouth onto a spoon and carry it to your plate.

If you have an accident at the table, such as spilled jelly, retrieve it with a utensil, and place it on your plate. You may wet a small corner of your napkin from your water glass and rub the spot lightly. Try to be as inconspicuous as possible and to relax. It happens to all of us.

Don't reach in front of others for something you want. Ask to have it passed, and be sure to say "please" and "thank you."

Accept food that is passed with your right hand, and pass it on with the left.

Turn a pitcher's handle toward the person receiving it.

Use implements provided in a serving dish. Never use your own utensils or your fingers.

Finger foods go from the serving plate to your plate, not directly to your mouth.

Break bread or rolls into small pieces before buttering.

Break or cut whole fruit.

Butter and jelly go on your bread-and-butter plate if one is used.

No toothpicks in public, ever! If you have food caught in your teeth, excuse yourself and remove it in privacy.

Don't play with the flatware.

If you must decline a food, simply say, "No, thank you." Avoid telling your hostess that you don't like something. If you are allergic to a certain food, quietly explain to your hostess.

Catch a sneeze in your handkerchief, never in your napkin.

Keep hands away from face and hair.

Don't try to retrieve dropped flatware. Politely ask for another piece.

It's an insult to the cook to shake salt or pepper over food you haven't tasted.

Hold a cup with your index finger through the handle, the thumb above it to support the grip. It's incorrect to "cradle" your cup if it has a handle. Keep the little finger down!

Test hot liquids by sipping quietly from a spoon.

Take modest portions of food.

If you burp, say (to no one in particular), "Excuse me!"

If a bug crawls out of your salad, ignore it and leave your salad untouched. This also applies to other foods on your plate.

If you must leave the table, for any reason, simply say, "Please excuse me for a moment."

Share conversation with all seated around you. It's rude to converse with only one person the entire meal.

Touch nothing on the table prior to saying grace.

Don't drink any liquid with food in your mouth.

Don't put the entire bowl of the spoon into your mouth.

Don't dunk food into a beverage.

Don't cleanse an olive pit from a large olive in your mouth. Take bites from it, and place it on your plate.

Don't drink bottled or canned drinks at a table; pour them into glasses. Reserve drinking from them for picnics.

Eat crisp bacon with fingers but softer bacon with a fork.

Use a fork for chicken and for french fried potatoes, however crisp, unless at a picnic.

Cut and eat only one piece of food at a time.

Don't leave any food on a spoon when you remove the spoon from your mouth.

Don't let a spoon stand in a glass or cup.

Don't reach for water as soon as you are seated. (It indicates nervousness.)

Pour gravy only on the meat, not on all the food on your plate.

Techniques for special foods

Cake. You may pick up small individual cakes, such as petits fours, with your fingers. Eat servings of cake with a fork.

Casserole (individual). If it is served on a plate, set it to the left and spoon portions onto your plate. As you finish each portion, take another if you wish. It is all yours.

Celery and radishes. Place these on your bread-and-butter plate, and eat them with the fingers.

Dip. Handle the chip gently so as not to break it in the dip. Don't re-dip with the same chip.

Eggs. *Fried egg*—Should be cut and eaten one piece at a time. Use a piece of bread on your fork for remaining egg yolk. *Soft-boiled egg*—Usually served in an egg cup. Crack the shell with the blade of the knife in a horizontal position. Take off the top with your fingers, season the egg in the shell, and eat it with a spoon. *Hard-cooked egg*—Rarely is it served in a shell. If it is, break the shell gently with your knife, remove the shell with your fingers, and cut the egg, one piece at a time, as you eat it.

Fruit. *Apple or pear*—Cut the fruit in quarters, and eat it with your fingers or with a fruit knife and fork. *Berries*—If they are served from a bowl, eat them with a spoon. If whole strawberries are served, hold them by the stem and eat the whole berry, or if they are very large, bite them in half. *Fresh, with pits*—Hold fruit in your fingers, and bite the meat of the fruit off the pit. If you put the pit into your mouth, remove it with your fingers. *Fruit salad*—Eat it with a spoon, not a fork. *Grapes*—When served, take or cut off a small bunch. Cut the grape with the point of your knife and remove the seeds, or put the whole grape into your mouth and drop the seeds into your hand (almost a fist). *Melon*—If it's cut into small pieces, use a spoon. Use a fork with watermelon served in slices (except at picnics!). *Orange*—Slit the rind with a sharp knife from top to bottom. Remove the rind with your fingers, and pull sections apart, eating one at a time.

Gravy. Ladle gravy onto the meat, potatoes, or rice. Do not pour it. It is correct to make a small indentation in the potatoes before ladling the gravy onto them. Bread may be sopped in the gravy if it is done one small piece at a time and eaten with a fork.

Meat. Chicken—You may eat it with the fingers in a casual setting, such as picnics. However, chicken served any other place should be handled with a knife and fork. *Chops*—Use a knife and fork. *Shish kebab*—Hold the skewer in one hand and remove the pieces onto your plate with your fork. Eat each piece with a fork, using your knife if necessary. Lay the skewer across your plate—never on the tablecloth.

Parsley and garnishes. Use a fork to eat them as part of the main dish.

Pickles. Eat sliced pickles from your plate with a fork, but it's acceptable to eat whole, small pickles with your fingers.

Pizza. You may eat this informal food with the fingers.

Potato (baked). Slit the top of the potato to season and butter. Use your fork to mix the seasonings. You may use your left hand to steady the potato. If it's served in foil, unfold the foil, but don't remove it entirely. If you choose to eat the skin, carefully cut and eat one piece at a time.

Sandwich. This should be cut, halved or quartered. If it's an open-face with sauce, use a knife and fork. Eat a club sandwich with the fingers. If you can't manage it, use a knife and fork.

Shrimp. Small shrimp served as a cocktail in sauce are eaten whole. Use a knife to cut jumbo shrimp served on a plate or a fork if in a shrimp cup. Shrimp served with tails may be held by the tail or by a fork and cut on the plate. Shrimp in the shell are removed from the shell and eaten with the fingers. A small cocktail fork may be provided. When finished, place the fork on the plate holding the shrimp cup. The hostess may provide a small individual dish for the shells. If not, keep them on your plate.

Spaghetti. It takes practice to eat spaghetti correctly. It shouldn't be cut. Instead, wind it around your fork, using the bowl of a large spoon in your other hand to support it. The spoon remains on your plate while you use the fork to put the food in your mouth.

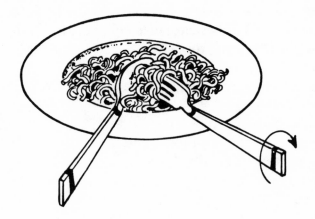

Tea. Tea should be served in a pot. But if it is served with the bag in the cup, remove the bag with your spoon, and place it on the saucer beside the cup.

How long to stay

Watch the hostess for a signal to leave the table. Compliment the hostess and offer to help clear the table. The dishes may be removed from either right or left; just remember not to reach across anyone.

The length of time you stay after a meal should be no less than forty minutes to an hour after a dinner. (Don't leave before the guest of honor departs.) After a brunch, an hour is sufficient, and a half hour to an hour is appropriate after a lunch.

Chapter 8

Challenges

1. Why are good table manners important?

2. What can table manners say about a person?

3. What advice can you give to someone who is invited to a dinner party but hesitates to accept because of uncertainty about how to eat properly?

4. How many rules for eating with poise can you remember? List them.

5. How is consideration for others shown at a buffet dinner or reception? Explain.

9

Setting the Table

*B*e hospitable to one another without grumbling"
(1 Peter 4:9).

An attractive table creates a pleasant atmosphere for dining. Fine silver and china are not necessary. A little imagination and color can produce a beautiful table set with the simplest flatware and dinnerware. For instance, a floral centerpiece with candles can be uninteresting, but a very pretty table was set for a luncheon by using a little bird's nest (artificial) with tiny candy eggs next to two clay pots of flowers. Lots of ideas will work effectively. You can even be daring and mix different china patterns and linens. There are some logistics, however, to remember in setting a table, which is something every young man and woman should know.

Formal vs. informal

Many young people ask the difference between formal and informal. You may use the same linens, dinnerware, and flatware for either, but formal generally means more of everything. More courses are served requiring more dinnerware, more glasses, more flatware.

The tablecloth is usually a conservative white linen or damask (a white on white pattern); the dinnerware is china; and the flatware is silver. Larger napkins are also used.

An informal table setting may be more colorful and more creative, and it requires fewer pieces of dinnerware, glassware, and flatware.

The tablecloth

There are many tablecloths from which to choose. Many are in beautiful prints and colors, and your choice should depend upon the dinnerware you use. There should be harmony in color and with the settings. For example, you should not use heavy pottery or earthenware (however beautiful) on a lace tablecloth. Lace somehow seems to call for bone china and crystal.

The middle crease of the cloth must be straight from one end of the table to the other end. The cloth should hang down about eighteen inches on all sides. If the table is oval, an oval cloth should be used. The cloth for a buffet table should go to the floor. This may be a bit impractical (or impossible) for most homes, but if the buffet table is in a place other than a home, you can see how a short cloth would detract from a beautifully set buffet table.

Table linens are made to be enjoyed, and with today's detergents you don't have to worry about spots. Plastic or vinyl is taboo, except at home and with family. If place mats are used, they should be evenly spaced and about one inch from the table edge.

The napkin

Napkins, too, come in many beautiful colors and can match the tablecloth or be in contrast, perhaps picking up a color in the centerpiece.

Napkins are placed to the left of the fork unless there is a service or place plate. (A service or place plate is the plate that is before you when you are seated at a formal dinner. It remains in front of you for the appetizer and soup and is re-

Absence of grace
and inharmonious movement
and discord
are nearly allied to ill works
and ill nature,
as grace and harmony
are the sisters and images
of goodness and virtue.

     —Plato, *The Republic*

moved when the main, "hot" course is served on another plate. The napkin is placed in the center of the service plate.) It is now fashionable to be creative with napkins, even crushing them gently into an empty goblet. Avoid paper napkins for indoors. It's better to use inexpensive drip-dry, if possible. However, if cloth napkins are used for the family, it's a good idea to use individual napkins rings to save laundry for Mother.

If a napkin is very large (formal dinner napkin, about twenty-four inches square), it is folded in half and then folded three times.

DINNER NAPKIN

If it is a smaller napkin (luncheon), it should be folded in the same manner but will require only two folds after it is folded in half.

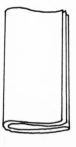

LUNCHEON NAPKIN

The centerpiece

There are no hard and fast rules about a centerpiece. Flowers or fruit are always appropriate, especially if they are fresh. Silk flowers are acceptable, but please do not use plastic flowers or wax fruit. A centerpiece should be colorful, perhaps picking up the colors in the dinnerware or the napkins. It should be in the center of the table, low enough that guests can see over it.

Candlelight is pleasant. Candles can be used as part of a centerpiece, but they shouldn't be lighted until late afternoon or early evening. Candles may be used on a luncheon table but not lit during daylight hours.

Flatware

Flatware is placed one inch or so from the edge of the table. All the flatware needed for the meal should be placed on the table. The pieces needed first are placed to the farthest right and left of the plate. There are usually two forks on the left, one for salad and one for meat, and a knife and two spoons to the right. Individual butter knives, if used, are usually placed across the top of the bread-and-butter plate.

If individual salt and pepper shakers are used, they are placed above each plate or between two persons. Otherwise, salt and pepper shakers should be strategically placed within reach for everyone.

Afternoon tea

The afternoon tea is a good idea when introducing someone new to your school or honoring some occasion. And, yes, young men *do* go to teas.

The table should be covered with a cloth. There should be no doilies on the trays used for coffee and tea services. On the tea tray with the teapot and hot water pot, be sure to have sugar, cream, and thinly sliced lemons. On the coffee tray, have the coffee serving pot, cream, and sugar. The serving pots are filled in the kitchen.

The cups and saucers and napkins should be arranged along the sides of the table and finger food in the center of the table. If saucers are omitted, use salad plates and place cups on the plates.

Today's rules are practical, but it does help to know where to place everything.

A separate table should be provided for all used china. Used china should not be placed on the serving table.

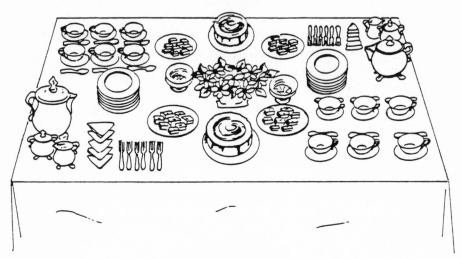

AFTERNOON TEA

The buffet

A buffet table is generally set more informally than a sit-down dinner and is much less work for the hostess. If small tables are made available for the guests, they may be preset with napkins, flatware, salt and pepper shakers, and perhaps butter. If not, all of these should be available at the buffet table.

At a buffet, the dessert may be served from the main buffet table, but all main course foods should be removed before the dessert is placed on the table. Coffee and tea are generally served from the main table or from a separate table.

BUFFET DINNER

The place setting

Each meal has its own dishes, glassware, and flatware to be set in a certain way. Today's rules are practical, but it does help to know where to place everything. The place setting, or grouping before each person, is illustrated below for each of the different occasions.

The setting you will use most often will be for an informal sit-down meal. Set the table like this:

TABLE SETTING FOR INFORMAL MEAL

All the flatware up to the dessert course is placed in the order in which it is used, from the outside working toward the plate. If soup is to be served, soup cups are placed on small (dessert) plates and soup spoons are at the far right. Substitute teaspoons if you plan to serve fruit instead, or salad forks to the far left if the first course is going to be salad.

The table setting for breakfast will look like this:

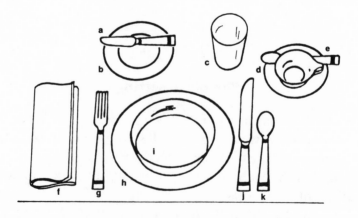

TABLE SETTING FOR BREAKFAST

a. Butter spreader (may also be placed vertically across the right side of this plate).
b. Bread-and-butter plate (primarily for informal meals). Jelly, bread, and butter are placed here.
c. Water glass.
d. Cup and saucer.
e. Teaspoon (on the saucer as shown, or at the right of the knife).
f. Napkins.
g. Fork.
h. Breakfast plate.
i. Cereal bowl.
j. Knife (always turned toward the plate or toward the diner).
k. Cereal spoon.

The luncheon setting will be as follows:

TABLE SETTING FOR LUNCHEON

a. Butter spreader.
b. Bread-and-butter plate.

c. Dessert spoon and fork, shown in the continental manner; equally correct is to bring these utensils in on the dessert plate with the fork to the left and the spoon to the right.

d. Water goblet.

e. Salad fork.

f. Meat fork.

g. Lunch plate.

h. Napkin.

i. Meat knife.

j. Soup spoon (round shape is correct with soup cups).

(NOTE: When coffee is served, the spoon is placed on the saucer, to the right of the cup. If iced tea is served, the iced-tea spoon goes to the right of the knife, but it is to remain on the coaster when one is finished.)

For a formal dinner, set each place as follows:

TABLE SETTING FOR FORMAL DINNER

a. Water goblet.

b. Fish fork.

   c. Salad fork.
   d. Meat fork.
   e. Service plate (always removed when main course is served; you don't eat from it).
   f. Napkin.
   g. Dinner knife.
   h. Salad knife.
   i. Fish knife.
   j. Soup spoon.
(NOTE: There is so much silverware on the table at a formal dinner that the dessert pieces are brought in with dessert.)

Wine glasses are also placed on a formal table to the right and lower than the water glass. A very formal dinner may have four glasses in addition to the water glass. They are (a) champagne, (b) red wine, (c) white wine, and (d) sherry.

Coffee is served after the meal, and the silver needed will be brought in with the coffee. The spoon is placed on the saucer.

Finger bowls

A finger bowl is rarely seen nowadays, except in a household with domestic staff or after lobster is served. It may be brought in on the dessert plate with a doily underneath and the dessert silverware on the plate. Remove the dessert fork and lay it at the left of your plate and the dessert spoon at the right. Lift the finger bowl and doily together, and set them on the table above the fork. If there is a small plate under the finger bowl, lift it with the bowl, also.

After dessert, dip the tips of the fingers of one hand at a time into the water, then dry them on your napkin, in your lap. If your mouth feels sticky, you may moisten your fingertips and dab your lips, then dry them with a quick pat of your napkin.

Place cards

Place cards may be unnecessary at a small party, but if they are decorated, they can be an attractive detail to carry out a party theme. Place cards are genuinely helpful in seating a large party. Write the guests' names as you usually use them, using first names or nicknames. Add the last names or initials if there are two guests with the same first name.

A single card should be laid flat on the napkin or above the plate. Folded cards or cards in little holders stand just above the plate. It is best to use holders of good quality, such as silver or china, designed in good taste.

For a formal dinner, use only plain white cards, placing them on the napkin or above the plate. Place cards with gold beveled edges are acceptable and attractive, also. Write names with titles (Miss Thompson, Mr. Edgars, Mrs. Smith-Jones) in black ink. At a club or hotel, place cards may be provided as part of the service. Ask to see them to be sure they are of good quality and taste.

Chapter 9

Challenges

1. Setting a beautiful table has been important to Americans—even the colonists. Why?

2. How do the beauty and orderliness of the dining table fit into the pattern of the Christian home?

3. Should the way a dining table looks and a meal is served be as important to the man of the house as it should be to the woman?

4. What role should the children in a home (particularly teens) play in coordinating beauty and proper procedure at mealtime? Explain.

10

The Looking Glass

Being well-groomed is important for many reasons. Good grooming affects the way you feel about yourself, gives you the confidence you exude, and underlines the "statement" you are making with your appearance. That statement tells others about you, as much or as little as you want them to know.

Most young people have times when they feel confident and other times when they don't. Wrinkled, ill-fitting clothes, unkempt nails, dirty hair, rundown shoes, all make them feel even more awkward.

Young men often get the idea that grooming is a "women only" concern. But that's not true! The masculine look is *clean* and *neat*. Shirts should be crisp and fresh. Dress and casual pants must have a crease. Jeans need to be clean.

Being well-groomed isn't a guarantee for success, but it's a giant step in that direction. Feeling comfortable and attractive is a big plus.

Neither weight nor size affects good grooming. Young people place much too much emphasis on size. Good looks depend entirely upon you and what you do with yourself. Good grooming is number one; after that, dress in what is becoming to you.

Most people (if they are honest) feel they have some physical flaw, such as a too-big nose, thin legs, too-short

143

arms—the list is endless. Much has been written by cosmetic companies and clothing designers, to say nothing of the companies that sell diet products to assist you in eliminating or concealing what you consider a physical flaw. If you feel you are overweight, you should seek assistance, as you should with any health problem. Health is of the essence. To be healthy, well groomed, and polite is your passport to social success.

Everyday steps to good grooming

1. *Take a daily bath or shower.*
2. *Apply deodorant.*
3. *Keep hair clean and neat.* Shampoo frequently and use a conditioner. Keep hair trimmed and styled.
4. *Use a razor.* Young men, if you shave, make it close. Stubble is unattractive. Young women, keep legs and underarms smooth. Don't be afraid of the razor. There are various kinds, all designed to keep you free from nicks and cuts.
5. *Maintain fresh breath.* Is there anything worse than bad breath? Keep your teeth clean, and always keep some mints on hand just in case.
6. *Manicure nails regularly.* It has been said that nails and shoes tell how neat and clean you really are. This applies to young men as well as to young women. Keep nails short and clean, and file them into an oval shape. If you bite your nails, seek help in breaking the habit. Long nails may seem glamorous to some young women, but they are not in good taste, nor are designs and dark or brightly colored polish. Give yourself some personal time every month with a pedicure. Ever notice how ugly toenails can be? They can be as attractive as your fingernails. It takes just a little extra time. Use a bit of polish on them, too.
7. *Make sure clothing is clean and pressed.* Ill-fitting clothing, especially too-tight clothing, is inappropriate. Keep shoes polished and in good shape; check heels and soles to see if they need repair.

The world is a looking glass
and gives back to every man
the reflection of his own face.

—William Thackeray

8. *Coordinate colors.*

9. *If you wear makeup, young women should apply makeup modestly and carefully.* Too much makeup or makeup in dramatic shades is certainly wrong for you.

10. *Wear your hair in a style that is becoming to you.* Avoid fads in hairstyles.

Dressing appropriately

Dressing appropriately and looking well-dressed go hand in hand. Your looks reveal your culture, your background, your values, your attitudes—just about everything there is to know about you. Your looks send a message. Looking good on Sunday but not on Monday creates conflicting impressions. This is not to say that what you wear to church on Sunday should be worn to school or the office on Monday. This is where "appropriate dress" enters the picture.

You can be well-dressed all the time if you are well-groomed and dressed appropriately for whatever the occasion, be it a wedding or a fishing trip. Clothing manufacturers provide vast selections for all requirements. The best-dressed people know how to take the most becoming elements of current fashion and fit them into their own style and budget.

Dressing yourself well is an art. Some people have more of a flair for it than others, but anyone can learn, with a little time and thought given to it. It has nothing to do with cost or name brands. It's a matter of knowing yourself and being able to select fashion trends and colors that are becoming to you. Longer or shorter skirts may be the high-fashion fad but may be totally unbecoming to some young women.

When you select clothing, consider the appearance of the total person and avoid attention-getting garments. This may mean you will have to throw out or let out those tight slacks and skirts or those thin, see-through blouses or shirts. These items of clothing draw unwanted attention and are in poor taste. Weed out unbecoming clothing. Consider what you have that goes together. Purchase only what you like, and give all purchases careful consideration. Garish colors and fad clothing made popular by so-called entertainment artists are out of character for the young person desirous of identity with Christ. The same applies to hairstyles for both young men and women. It is regrettable that some young men actually appear to desire an effeminate appearance with permed hair and gold jewelry.

Consider the appearance of the total person and avoid attention-getting garments.

"The fashion of this world passeth away" (1 Corinthians 7:31 KJV).

Psychologists confirm that clothing affects the personality. Your attitude and actions are determined in part by the way you are dressed. Organizations requiring uniforms do so for conformity and authority as well as for appearance. Many private schools have battled pressure to relax the shirt-and-tie requirement for young men. These schools have maintained the position that proper attire fosters proper behavior, and they have also found that proper attire contributes to the self-discipline necessary for outstanding academic performance.

Message clothing

It may surprise you, but most fashion analysts agree that fashion designers tend to design clothing to send social and political messages. For many years there has been a revolt worldwide against our American culture and tradition, and the attitude is often expressed through faded, washed-out, wrinkled, tight-fitting, sensual clothing. It is not just the appearance of the clothing, but *where it is worn*. Acceptance has come slowly, but today this type of clothing is everywhere, even on church ushers and on choir members. It's a subtle way of saying, "I'm going to be me, regardless . . ." But what is really being said is that the "me" has joined the ranks of the current culture with the message it is sending. Many Christians in an effort to just "fit in" with the crowd or to be comfortable are not at all aware of this.

New fashions and colors are fun and exciting and may be appropriate for your clothing needs. However, because today's clothing styles, particularly for young people, go beyond what looks or feels good, it is extremely important to your Christian image that you take a good, even second, look in the mirror and ask yourself, "Would Christ approve?" Parents may have something to say, too. Show respect to them, listen and obey. This pleases God.

A prestigious eastern school allowed young men to wear faded jeans with quality sports jackets, shirts, and ties. As authority declined, so did adherence to what has been traditionally correct attire. There has been a recent trend back to tradition, and fashionable finishing schools are now in vogue again.

You must use discernment in all areas. It's never easy to go contrary to the world, but if the timeless, unchanging, godly principles have governed your life in everything else, in the matter of dress, too, you'll be a winner!

What to wear when

For informal occasions such as parties, social and school events, games, shopping, dining out at an informal restaurant, or dining in a private home on an informal occasion with everyday table settings, the appropriate dress is as follows:

Informal occasions

For young men:
- sports jacket, open shirt
- sports jacket, shirt, and tie
- sweater over open-necked shirt

For young women:
- dresses
- culottes
- good slacks with shirt or sweater

- sweater over shirt and tie
- dress jeans
- good slacks
- *no* worn jeans, T-shirts, work clothes, or shorts

- good jeans with shirt or sweater
- suit with blouse or sweater
- skirt and blouse
- *no* worn jeans, T-shirts, work clothes, or shorts

Formal occasions, such as weddings, formal dinner parties, or debutante coming-out parties, may also be black-tie occasions. The appropriate dress for these functions is as follows:

Formal occasions

For young men:
- tuxedo (if noted on the invitation)
- white tie (if noted on the invitation)
- black bow tie
- formal dinner jacket
- formal trousers
- white linen jacket (in summer)
- white shirt with stud buttons
- a waistcoat or cummerbund
- black socks and black shoes
- dress suit, white shirt, conservative tie

For young women:
- full-length evening or dinner dress
- very dressy dress (below the knee length)
- heels (always hose to go with them)
- evening bag
- *no* pantsuits
- *no* outerwear of clashing color
- *no* low-cut or strapless gown

Timely tips for young women

If you are tall, avoid skirts that are too long. If you are short, avoid short skirts; they give you a square look. Long lines with one-color harmony will give the effect of height.

If you are slim, you can wear contrasting colors. If you are very thin, you can wear bulky, weighty fabrics, but no loosely fitting clothing. Obviously, if you are heavier, you should avoid bulky fabrics and concentrate on using longer lines and a one-color look; don't wear contrasting colors and horizontal lines. If you have heavy legs, wear substantial heels. Thin heels accentuate a heavy leg.

How to sit, walk, stand

Visual poise is essential to the image of the capable and attractive young person. Posture is paramount. Sitting gracefully, walking smoothly, and standing erectly are abilities to be desired by everyone. With only a little practice, they are attainable. If physical irregularities make them impossible, a radiant expression and a positive attitude will compensate. Many people in wheelchairs are the essence of poise.

When seating yourself, walk directly to the chair (maintaining good posture as you walk), glance down at the chair, turn and lower yourself in one fluid motion without looking again at the chair. Don't use the chair for support. Young women shouldn't smooth their dresses with their hands (or even one hand) as they sit down; if straightening must be done, ease it out slightly from the side. Slide back into the seat as much as possible and relax.

Place your hands in your lap or one hand in your lap and one on the arm of the chair. Young women may want to have both hands in their laps with palms up and one hand resting on the other. Try to avoid needless motions with your hands.

It is more attractive and graceful to cross legs at the ankles, keeping the knees together than to cross legs above the knees. Crossing legs above the knees also restricts circulation, often causing tiny veins to break.

Young men shouldn't cross their legs at all or rest an ankle on a knee. Sit with feet flat on the floor, knees apart just a comfortable distance, and back straight.

To sit on the floor, a young woman may place her left

foot above left of the right, bending the left knee as she kneels on the right knee. As she sits back toward her heels, she can slide her seat to the right and her feet to the left. It is helpful to sit with one hand on the floor for balance. Young men may want to bend their knees up to their chests with arms around their knees for balance. To get up, young women may rise to their knees, put their weight onto one foot, and rise.

To seat yourself in a theater seat, don't look at the seat. Simply use your hand to lower it and be seated.

When you are walking, hold your head high, following a smooth line. Don't bob up and down. Your shoulders should be almost motionless. Keep your arms close to your body; they should swing easily from your shoulders. Take short, appropriate steps, lifting (not scuffing) each foot and placing it in front of you. Your height will determine the length of your step. A short person naturally wouldn't take the same steps as a person with longer legs. Keep your knees relaxed and feet parallel to each other. Avoid the "paddle-walk" (toes out) with which we are all familiar. Walking with poise says a lot about you, and it will make you feel good about yourself, too.

Much of your life is spent standing. You can look and feel "all arms" or "all legs," or you can be confident in any standing position. It's up to you. Posture is the key. It's essential to good looks and good health. Poor posture is the enemy against which neither beautiful clothing nor a well-proportioned body can compete. So stand straight, head high, and shoulders back.

Young women, the model stance is the "clock" stance—the right foot pointed to twelve and the left, instep to right heel, to ten. This is the most socially acceptable stance. It looks good in photographs, too. If the clock stance is uncomfortable for you, you may prefer simply to point both feet forward. The important thing is that you look relaxed and poised.

If you must fold your arms, be sure one hand is showing.

It is not a pretty sight to see both hands tucked under your arms. This applies to young men as well as to young women.

You've heard the saying, "It's the little foxes that spoil the vine"? Well, this happens to be true in just too many areas of life.

Eric, a handsome young aide to a U.S. senator in Washington, D.C., was dressed to perfection for his role in the United States Senate building. He stepped into the elevator one day carrying a black leather briefcase. He wore a pin-striped suit, a white shirt, and a silk tie, but his shoes? A total disaster! The heels were worn down, and they had never seen polish.

Mary was hired, directly from high school, as a secretary for a law firm. She was trim, always well dressed, and neat— except for her nails! The nail polish was a shade or two too dark, the polish chipped, and the nails too long.

You may not realize what a negative effect these "little" things can have on your image.

The 20 worst image destroyers for young women

1. Unpolished shoes with worn-down heels.
2. Nylons with runs or reinforced toes in open-style shoes.
3. Oily, unkempt hair.
4. Makeup stained collars.
5. Lint or dandruff on clothing.
6. Underarm stains or odor.
7. Missing buttons, snaps, or hooks or noticeable safety pins.
8. Too heavy makeup.
9. Noticeable lingerie straps or slips showing.
10. Visible bra or panty lines.
11. Lack of necessary undergarments (some are *always* necessary).
12. Linings that hang below the garment hem.
13. Coats too short.

14. Skirts or slacks too tight and ill-fitting.
15. Jacket sleeve length too long or short (should be to the wristbone).
16. Blouses gaping at bustline.
17. Garments that look worn, pilled, frayed, faded, or stained.
18. Unmanicured nails or chipped nail polish.
19. Uncoordinated colors or patterns in clothing.
20. Inappropriate jewelry (wrong colors, too heavy, or too dressy).

The 20 worst image destroyers for young men

1. Unpolished or rundown shoes.
2. Socks not long enough to cover leg when sitting or not coordinated in color to trousers.
3. Unshaven face.
4. Soiled or wrinkled collars.
5. Lint or dandruff on clothing.
6. Missing buttons or belt loops or broken zippers.
7. Linings that hang below garment hem.
8. Jackets too short or improper sleeve length.
9. Trousers with no crease.
10. Trousers too short or too long.
11. Shirts unbuttoned to reveal chest.
12. Clothes that look worn, pilled, frayed, faded, or stained.
13. Oily, unkempt hair.
14. Trousers too tight.
15. Nails not cut and/or unclean.
16. Improper selection of shoes (such as sneakers with suit).
17. Dirty handkerchief.
18. Uncoordinated colors.
19. Underarm stains or odor.
20. Spots on clothing.

Chapter 10

Challenges

1. Much emphasis is put on good grooming and appearance. In your opinion, why?

2. What is "message" clothing? Give examples.

3. What should the Christian young person's attitude be toward "message" clothing?

4. What factors should be considered in dressing for a job interview? (Refer to chapter 4.) Why?

5. How important is good posture? Why?

6. Check your memory on "Don't Ruin Your Image." How many points can you list?

Communication—
A Lost Art Found

Everyone enjoys receiving mail, but in this busy world of ours, we too often neglect letter writing. To people away from home, a letter is the next best thing to a visit. A letter can be read and savored over and over again.

Correspondence

Your letters reflect you; therefore, you should take care that they reflect a "you" of which you can be proud. Never write a letter expressing anger or disgust. Write nothing for which you will later be sorry. Your attitude, your spirit, may change, but what you put in writing lasts forever. Most letters can be typewritten, but three types of letters must always be handwritten: formal notes and replies; sympathy (condolence) letters; and thank-you notes.

A wide choice of stationery is available today, and there are no hard and fast rules for informal letters. Men avoid colors and generally use white, ivory, or gray paper. There are, of course, some "rules of the game" for business letters.

Printed or engraved paper is often given as a gift. Engraving is expensive but very attractive. If only your name is used, you can use the paper for a long time, even if your address changes. Don't use metallic printing or borders. The second sheet should be plain.

The proper printing form, depending on your choice, would be the following:

- Name centered at the top
- Address only, centered at the top
- Name and address (one line at top center)
- Monogram in upper left-hand corner

Three kinds of paper will cover almost all informal correspondence. Folded or plain sheets may be used. If you use folded sheets, be sure to number the pages. As you slip a letter into the envelope, keep open edges to the top with the salutation facing the reader as the letter is taken from the envelope.

If you use a single sheet, fold it in thirds. Neatly fold the top third down first and then the bottom over it. Put it into the envelope in that manner.

To meet all your correspondence needs (formal and informal), you should have the following on hand:

- *Informal paper for letters*. This may be single or folded sheets, in the colors of your choice.
- *Paper for formal occasions,* such as answering formal invitations and writing letters of sympathy. This paper should be white or off-white. It could be plain or have a monogram. Use black or dark blue ink.
- *Postal cards*. These are for short messages. They can also be for invitations or greetings. They come in various colors and may be printed with your name and address.
- *Correspondence cards*. If you don't like writing letters, these are for you. The card is about 4-by-5 inches and has an envelope. Your name and address or just your name or initials may be at the top. They may be in a color or white.
- *Note paper*. This is usually 3$1/2$-by-5 inches and folded (doubled). The fold is at the top. Note paper may be printed with your name and address or monogrammed. Very attractive note paper is also available

This is the beginning of a new day.
God has given me this day to use as I will.
I can waste it or grow in its light
and be of service to others.
I can write a letter, speak a soft word.
What I do with this day is important
because I have exchanged a day of my life for it.
When tomorrow comes, today will be gone forever.
I hope I will not regret the price I paid for it.

through stationery stores and card shops. It is used for short messages or invitations.

- *Informals*. An informal is usually white or ivory and is always doubled over. It is about 3-by-4 or 4-by-4½ inches. There may be a raised panel border. Your name should be engraved in the center of the front. It is used for thank-you notes, invitations, or gift enclosures.

Personal letters

As you begin a personal letter, you may write your address in the upper right-hand corner with the date below or just the date alone.

Begin with the salutation, "Dear Mary," or if you want to be formal, "My Dear Mrs. Jones" with a comma following it. (*Dear* is a polite salutation for business as well as personal letters. It is not a term of endearment when used in this way.) After the body of the letter, simply use a closing, such as "Sincerely," "Fondly," or "Love," using a comma, and then sign your name. The closing will depend on your relationship to the person to whom you are writing.

000 Street	return address
City, State Zip	
Month 00, 19—	date
Dear Louise,	salutation
The letter with your travel plans arrived today. I'm so happy that you will be able to stay with us for a couple of days. What fun we'll have talking about "the good old days" yet to be!	body
Let me know when you'll be arriving, and we'll meet you at the airport.	
Love,	closing
Beth	signature

Business letters

Business letters should be written on plain, quality paper. They should be typed, but if that isn't possible, write them with a legible hand. You should sign all letters by hand. A business letter should have your address in the upper right-hand corner with the date below it.

The addressee's name in full, his/her title, and address should appear at the left of the page, a few lines below the line upon which you have written the date. Use no punctuation at the ends of the lines. If you know only the title of the person to whom you are writing, it is correct to use that. The salutation goes below the address, leaving a double space between. It should be flush with the margin.

After the body of the letter, use a formal closing, such as "Very truly yours," "Sincerely," or "Yours truly." Your name should be typed under the closing, but be sure to leave enough space to sign your name (usually three or four lines).

Always use an envelope that matches your paper. Address the letter block style or indent each line slightly.

Letters are an important part of our lives, and they bring joy to the people who receive them.

Always precede the name of an addressee on the envelope with a title, such as Miss, Mr. and Mrs., Mrs., or Mr. If a letter is addressed to two young women, it should be "Misses Jane and Sue Jones." If it is to two young men, it should be "Messrs. James and Bob Jones." If a boy is under thirteen, he is addressed as "Master."

Thank-you letters

Write thank-you letters within a week after you have received a gift or have been entertained. After all, gratitude and consideration of others are what good manners are all about. Being too busy is *no* excuse.

Party invitations

If you are sending out party invitations, send them two weeks in advance of the date. (See chapter 6: "Giving a Party" for more information.)

Formal invitations

Formal invitations should be sent for banquets, weddings, receptions, and other official functions. They should be sent at least two weeks in advance. The invitation itself indicates the formality of the occasion, but if the most formal attire is required, "White Tie" is printed in the lower right corner.

Letters of sympathy

Letters and cards of sympathy (condolence) are gestures of kindness, and they should be acknowledged. The message can be brief. It shows appreciation for the sympathy and understanding extended. Commercial cards selected for quality and content are also appropriate.

The "why" of correspondence

We've covered the "how-to" and the "what to use" in correct correspondence. However, don't let your lack of suitable paper hinder the need or impulse to correspond with someone. Letters are an important part of our lives, and they bring joy to the people who receive them. People away from home, in prison, in hospitals, need to know you care, and except for a personal visit, a letter is the best thing to convey your feelings to them. You can send your thoughts and feelings to the farthest corners of the globe. And you can relay the message of the light of life—Christ!

"And I appeal to you, brethren, bear with the word of exhortation, for I have written to you in few words" (Hebrews 13:22).

Conversation

A U.S. brokerage firm made this slogan popular: "When . . . speaks, everyone listens." Speech plays an important role in making friends. Your conversation says a lot about you and has a great deal to do with how interesting you are. You may be shy around people you want to impress and find conversation frustrating. However, you can learn to express yourself well and remedy any conversational worries you now have.

For all the talking we do, few of us have mastered the art of being a good conversationalist. There are a few things to learn and remember about conversing with someone if you want to be heard and understood. Conversation involves talking *and* listening. Consider the other person. A good conversationalist is first a good listener. Ask questions that indicate an interest in what he/she is saying. Use sincere compliments. Everyone loves praise.

When you are talking, avoid tedious details. These rob your story or conversation of interest, and the listener tends to lose your train of thought. A subject that interests you may not interest someone else—at least not to the same degree. Be observant. If you feel interest is waning in what you are saying, change the subject. Conversation involves at least one other person. Therefore, be aware of the "air time" you take. It isn't fair to do all the talking.

You will make a lot of points as a conversationalist if, when you sense someone is shy or frustrated in conversation, you stimulate his/her interest by bringing up subjects you know are of interest to him/her. Drawing conversation out of a shy person is helpful and considerate. When you are listening to someone else, keep a sense of humor, and if something is funny, a laugh shows you are paying attention.

You may feel you are a good conversationalist with your peers but fail with adults. Young people and adults are interested in the same subjects but may see them from a different point of view. Adults enjoy hearing about things that interest young people, and they are often flattered by a young person's desire to share conversation with them. In a group of adults, be sensitive to adult interests and respect their opinions. It's rude to contradict. Be polite and courteous in all conversation.

Try to learn how you sound when you speak. A tape recorder can be a vital tool in speech correction. Practice clear enunciation. If you have an accent, don't try to change it unless it hinders communication. Natural accents can be charming. Your voice should be pleasant, neither dictatorial nor overly sweet. Keep it clear and unaffected. Avoid the common errors of running words together (slurring), dropping letters and syllables, talking too loudly, and talking too fast. Let your speech match your image. If a course in public speaking is offered in your school, take advantage of it.

The way you enunciate your words is important. You may remember the story of *My Fair Lady* in which Eliza Doolittle, a street peddler, was taught correct enunciation and became a very proper lady. Concentrate on how you say your words. How much better it sounds to say "something" rather than "sump-thun" or "coming" instead of "comin'." Omitting the "-ing" from words robs our language of its beauty and lowers you in social esteem. A well-known expert in "success" behavior calls attention to such speech imperfections. He insists that a person's social status can be determined by speech. Try to say "you" instead of "ya" or "yuh." Don't limit yourself to a social class; your mission, as a Christian, rises high above social classes.

Talk is made of words, and it follows that the more words

you know, the better you'll be able to express yourself. As you read, look up words unfamiliar to you and use them in your conversation. Build your word power!

Speech patterns are contagious. Many trite, overworked expressions are familiar to all of us. Using them shows careless speech habits, and it's boring. Avoid overworking expressions and speech fads—"y'know"; "go for it"; "I mean"; "I like"; "all right"; "you've got to be kidding"; "neat"—the list goes on and on. Be original in your responses. Avoid too much slang. Be your own person.

Of course, you don't have to be reminded to exercise good judgment in any jokes you tell. Avoid jokes that belittle or put down other races or cultures.

"Let your speech always be with grace, seasoned with salt, that you may know how you ought to answer each one" (Colossians 4:6). *"A word fitly spoken is like apples of gold in settings of silver"* (Proverbs 25:11). *A word spoken in due season, how good it is!"* (Proverbs 15:23).

Chapter 11

Challenges

1. Can letter writing be used to carry out any of Christ's commandments? Explain.

2. When is a thank-you letter required?

3. What should a sympathy letter contain?

4. What makes a good conversationalist?

5. What are speech fads, and how should the Christian young person handle them?

6. How important is word power? How do you gain it?

I Pledge Allegiance

*L*et every soul be subject to the governing authorities. For there is no authority except from God, and the authorities that exist are appointed by God" (Romans 13:1)

Allegiance: what it means

"I pledge allegiance to the flag. . . ." How often we repeat those words. But do we really know what they mean?

Most Americans who travel overseas say the most exciting part of their trip was returning to the shores of the United States of America. The Statue of Liberty and the American flag seem to take on new meaning and significance. Senator Jeremiah Denton's first words upon returning home from a prisoner-of-war camp in Vietnam were "God bless America." He even stooped and kissed the ground. He expressed the real joy of freedom.

How sad that we take this precious gift so lightly. Perhaps the real value of freedom cannot be fully known until it has been denied. God forbid that we should experience that denial.

The freedom we now enjoy as a nation was won for us by the American Revolution (1775–1783). It has been guaranteed to us by our Constitution. Representatives from American states convened in Philadelphia in May 1787 to revise a document that, they hoped, would bring unity and order to their newly created nation. Four months later, on September 17, they delivered a document that laid the foundation for a truly democratic society, establishing a federal government *of* the people, *by* the people, and *for* the people.

Freedom is fragile, and it requires nurturing and protecting. There are, and always have been (according to God's Word), forces working determinedly to destroy freedom and the concept of a sovereign God. Some consider this to be the basis for opposition to prayer in public places. Recognizing God in public places strengthens the concept of a sovereign God. Those who think they prefer a more socialistic, humanistic form of government feel it necessary to destroy or minimize the idea of a God who rules over and governs humankind.

The responsibility of preserving our national freedom based on "In God We Trust" must be the collective responsibility of all Americans, and that includes young people.

How to help

Learn the basic structure of our government. You will see that it was developed by our forefathers to be truly "of the people." We can have a voice and an influence in all legislation.

Before you get involved with any group,
be sure you understand the goals
and philosophies of the organization.

Most states and communities have organizations to help young Americans learn more about their government and have an active role in it. However, before you get involved with any group, be sure you understand the goals and philosophies of the organization. Some subversive groups masquer-

Love of Country

Breathes there the man with soul so dead
Who never to himself hath said,
"This is my own, my native land!"
Whose heart hath ne'er within him burned,
As home his footsteps he hath turned
From wandering on a foreign strand?
If such there breathe, go, mark him well!
For him no minstrel raptures swell;
High though his titles, proud his name,
Boundless his wealth as wish can claim,—
Despite those titles, power, and pelf,
The wretch, concenter'd all in self,
Living, shall forfeit fair renown,
And, doubly dying, shall go down
To the vile dust from whence he sprung,
Unwept, unhonored, and unsung.

—Sir Walter Scott

ade under names that seem innocent and even patriotic. Ask your parents, teachers, and minister for guidance. Their discernment is important.

Involvement in a good political organization can be exciting and rewarding. You will meet other young people who share your political views. They may be from different races and religions, but your steadfast convictions can be a very positive influence on them and on legislation. You can express your beliefs on current issues such as abortion and AIDS.

Get acquainted with your state legislators as well as your U.S. congressmen and senators. Their telephone numbers are listed in your directory, and they welcome visits from constituents. They often have summer jobs available or can direct you to other jobs in government. These individuals are your elected representatives and are basically servants of the people. They can be of great help to you and your family in difficult situations where the government is involved—passports, visas, social security, student loans, and many others. They also make appointments to U.S. military academies. They have a staff of research people to help you at any time. Take advantage of this privilege. You will be richer and wiser for it.

The American flag

No book on correct social behavior would be complete without instruction on the honoring of our American flag. God ordained governments and commanded us to be obedient to them.

"Keep the king's commandment for the sake of your oath to God" (Ecclesiastes 8:2). *"Remind them to be subject to rulers and authorities, to obey, to be ready for every good work"* (Titus 3:1). *"Therefore submit yourselves to every ordinance of man for the Lord's sake"* (1 Peter 2:13). *"You shall not revile God, nor curse a ruler of your people"* (Exodus 22:28).

Our flag should be given a very special place in our hearts. All that we enjoy today was earned for us by those who fought and perhaps died in defense of our flag and the freedoms for which it stands. Shouldn't our hearts swell with pride and perhaps our eyes become moist as we see unfurled what to us is the most beautiful flag in the world? Do you remember the words of the song: "This is my country, to have and to hold"? We may sing it without thought, but "holding" our country is a battle that is fought every day in many ways.

It isn't the purpose of this chapter to provide details on how our freedom was won and is maintained, but let it suffice to say that our nation, with the freedom we know, was purchased at a great price. Because our flag is the very symbol of our freedom, we display it and proudly give honor to it. There are, however, some regulations regarding the proper display and honoring of our flag. They are as follows:

1. The flag is normally flown outdoors only during daylight hours. However, it may also be flown at night if it is lighted.
2. When the flag is hung against a wall, the union (blue field) of the flag should be upward and on the flag's own right.
3. When displayed with another flag against the wall, from crossed staffs, the flag of the United States should be on the flag's own right, with its staff in front of the other staff.
4. The flag should never be allowed to touch the ground or trail in the water or be used in any other way in which it would be soiled easily.
5. When the flag is carried with another flag, the flag of the United States should be at the right. When carried with two other flags, it should be in the center.
6. The flag at half-staff is a sign of mourning. When flown at half-staff, the flag should be raised to the peak for an

instant and then lowered to the half-staff position. It
should be raised again to the peak before lowering.

7. The flag flown upside down is a signal of distress.
8. The flag should always be allowed to hang free. It should
   never be used as drapery.
9. The law forbids use of the flag in connection with any
   merchandise for sale.
10. An old, torn, or soiled flag should not be thrown away; it
    may, however, be destroyed as a whole, as by burning it.
11. Two persons are required to fold an American flag cor-
    rectly. See the diagrams for correct folding. One person

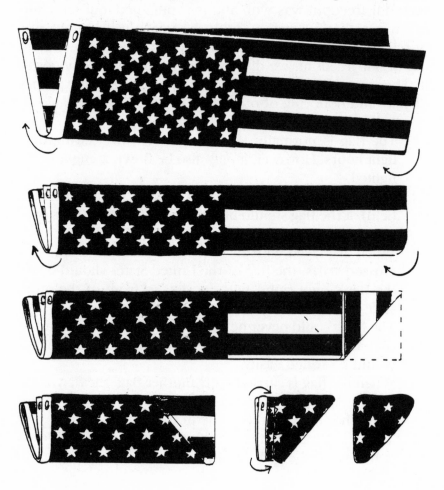

should hold the union (blue field) end while the other person does the folding.

12. On the following days the American flag is generally displayed in all parts of the United States: New Year's Day (January 1), Flag Day (June 14), Independence Day (July 4), Veterans Day (November 11), and Christmas Day (December 25). Dates vary for the observance of the following holidays: Lincoln's Birthday (first Monday in February), Washington's Birthday (third Monday in February), Mother's Day (second Sunday in May), Memorial Day (last Monday in May, at half-staff until noon), Labor Day (first Monday in September), Columbus Day (second Monday in October), and Thanksgiving Day (fourth Thursday in November).

When an invocation and a salute to the flag are given at a public meeting, the invocation always precedes the salute.

The national anthem

Rise immediately when the national anthem is played, and stand at attention. If you don't know the words, you should learn them. Even if you feel you aren't a singer, make an attempt to sing along and give proper honor to the country. If a young man is wearing a hat, he should remove it and hold it with his right hand over his heart. All others may place the right hand over the heart.

The Christian flag

The Christian flag was designed by Charles Overton in 1897 to symbolize Protestant Christianity. It is always a white flag bearing a red cross on a dark blue canton (the top inside quarter). It expresses Christian principles and is revered for its symbolism. Treat it with the same respect as the American flag. It should be displayed to the American flag's left.

Chapter 12

Challenges

1. What does "I pledge allegiance" mean to you?

2. How was our freedom won? How is it guaranteed?

3. List ways by which our freedom can be preserved.

4. In your opinion, what is the basis for the removal of prayer in public places?

5. How can young people get involved in government? Write out a step-by-step outline that can be followed.

6. What is the main responsibility of your elected officials?

7. How can your congressman and senators help you and your family personally?

8. Why do we put so much emphasis on our flag?

9. How do we give honor to our national anthem?

10. What is symbolized in the Christian flag?

America First

America first, not only in things material,
But in things of the spirit.
Not merely in science, invention, motors, skyscrapers,
But also in ideals, principles, character.
Not merely in the calm assertion of rights,
But in the glad assumption of duties.

Not flouting her strength as a giant,
But bending in helpfulness over a sick and wounded world
    like a good Samaritan.
Not in splendid isolation,
But in courageous cooperation.

Not in pride, arrogance, and disdain of other races and
    peoples,
But in sympathy, love, and understanding.
Not in treading again the old, worn, bloody pathway which
    ends inevitably in chaos and disaster,
But in blazing a new trail along which, please God, other
    nations will follow into the new Jerusalem where wars
    shall be no more.

Some day, some nation must take that path—unless we are
    to lapse into utter barbarism—and that honor I covet
    for my beloved America.
And so in that spirit and with these hopes, I say with all
    my heart and soul, "America First."

—G. Ashton Oldham

Appendix A
How to Have a Quiet Time

The "quiet time" is perhaps the most important part of your day as a Christian. When you establish a *daily* time set aside for meditation in God's Word, you will discover that every phase of your life and thinking will be changed. Your prayer life will be motivated, and your reading of the Word will take on new meaning. Your goals and motives will be lifted; you will find a "solid rock" in times of trouble and answers to those concerns of deep interest to you. Your hunger for souls will be increased and awakened; your code of Christian conduct will be sharper. Therefore, please establish a daily quiet time and cultivate it each day of your life.

Young people are often gripped with the concern, "How can I know God's will for me?" God reveals His will in three ways: through His Word, through prayer, and through circumstances. All three of these factors must come together. Too often young people in their zeal depend upon only one of the three, circumstances, and yet that factor is only reliable when combined with the other two factors. There may be nothing wrong with putting out a "fleece" like Gideon, but only if careful attention and *time* have been given to prayer and the reading of His Word.

Give priority to your quiet time when you arrange your schedule. Consistently observe the time you've chosen for your quiet time. It should be a convenient time of the day or night, as well as the quietest time possible.

Give attention to the procedure you use for your quiet

174

time. It should be more than just reading a few verses and praying a quick prayer. Try to include the following items:

1. Read God's Word.

2. Mark your Bible as you read. Use "sign language" to indicate your reactions, such as an exclamation point if you understand and appreciate, a question mark if you do not understand, a star or a key by verses with important truths or points.

3. Meditate on what you have read. Try to boil it down to one sentence. Look at the passage as Scripture presents it, and then try to see what He wants you to learn from it.

4. Remember that in Deuteronomy 6:7 there is a list of routine things you do every day during which you can think further about the Scriptures you have read—things like sitting in your house, walking somewhere, lying down, and getting up.

5. Apply some truth of the passage you have read to your own life. This is a continuation of your meditation, seeing what God has for *you* in His Word. If you have difficulty in finding an application, ask yourself these questions: Is there any example for me to follow? Is there any commandment for me to obey? Is there any sin for me to forsake? Is there any promise for me to claim?

6. Spend time in prayer. Prayer is not just asking for things; it is giving God adoration and praise, getting your heart right with Him by confessing recent sins, thanking God for answers He has given and for answers He is going to give, and then making known to Him in prayer the requests that you have for others as well as for yourself. You will want to keep a prayer list of requests for unsaved friends, for family, missionaries, and Christian friends. Put the dates you have prayed for each one, filling in how and when each prayer request was answered.

7. Try to share with someone else each day something you gained from your quiet time. This can be a real blessing for that person as well as for you.

Quiet time diaries and prayer calendars are available at local bookstores. Many young people like to keep a record of their reading and prayer requests. This writer cannot stress enough how meaningful a personal, private, quiet time will be for you—God is always there waiting.

Appendix B

Senior Adults— Grandparents

Grandparents are very special people. The Bible tells us to "rise in the presence of the aged, show respect for the elderly and revere your God" (Leviticus 19:32 NIV).

To those that honor the aged:

Blessed are those who understand my hesitant step and my trembling hand.

Blessed are those who know that today my ears will strain to hear them.

Blessed are those who seem to accept my failing eyesight and my spirit slowing down.

Blessed are those who turn their eyes when I spill my coffee at the table.

Blessed are those who, with a bright smile, stop to chat a while with me.

Blessed are those who never say, "That's the second time today you've told me that story."

Blessed are those who have the gift of helping me to remember the days gone by.

Blessed are those who have made me a person loved and respected and not abandoned.

Blessed are those who discern that I am no longer strong enough to bear my cross alone.

Blessed are those who soften by their love the days which remain to live until that last trip to the Father's house.

—Author Unknown

Appendix C
Principles of Music Evaluation

Music affects every area of our lives.* We hear it over the radio and through our stereo systems around home and in our automobiles. We have it forced into our ears by television, in banks, supermarkets, and modern malls. Everywhere we go, there is music. It is estimated that the average person spends forty-five hours a week watching television, but over ninety hours listening to music. As Christians, we need to discover our Lord's thoughts concerning music. Of the multibillion-dollar, record-related industries, over 75 percent is currently being spent on what is called popular or rock music. Slightly more than 5 percent is being spent on what is called Christian music.

How does rock music affect our lives? What is it saying? The message is threefold. *First, rock music is aimed at the spirit.* Its message is revolution. One of the current desires of American youths is to have real joy and happiness. Satan presents a false hope. Much of rock music gives youths today a false hope about hell. It is also continually overlaid with an attitude of antisociety, antipolice, and antijudicial system.

Second, rock music is aimed at the mind. Its message is drugs and suicide. Interestingly enough, the number-two desire of youths today is peace of mind. *People* magazine reported that in 1984, five thousand U.S. teens committed

*The material in this section is excerpted and adapted from Word of Life's "Rock Music" from the *Teen Student Manual*. Used by permission of Word of Life Fellowship, Inc.

suicide, and five hundred thousand attempted it—all in the wake of current rock songs encouraging listeners to welcome death as a way out of their problems.

Third, rock music is aimed at the body. Its message is sex. In one poll among several thousand American youths, the youths said that love was the number-one desire in their lives. Current popular songs carry the sexual message to your generation. Some songs are so vulgar they should be X-rated. Yet, one popular singer dedicates all his sexual songs to Deity. (The god of this world must be delighted.)

Dr. Allan Bloom, a professor on the Committee on Social Thought at the University of Chicago, states in his latest book, *The Closing of the American Mind,* that rock music has one appeal only, a barbaric appeal, to sexual desire—not love, not eros—undeveloped and untutored.

While you are listening to music, any kind, any time, ask yourself the following questions in evaluation:

- What was I thinking about as I heard this music?
- Did it affect my emotions? In what way?
- Did it inspire me spiritually?
- In what way did it inspire me?
- Would I want this music to be played on Sunday morning in church? Why or why not?
- Could I pray while listening to this music?
- Could I think while listening to this music?
- Is this music?

If we will remember that God's Word advises us to acknowledge Him in *all* our ways, we will recognize that what we listen to, what we fill our minds with, must be honoring to God before we can serve Him as He desires.

Appendix D
Tipping

Tipping for services rendered—*to* *i*nsure *p*romptness—is a part of our American life. Some people's livelihood depends upon the tips they receive. There is a long list of persons for whose services tipping is expected. How much to tip can be determined by inquiring from business persons where you live or visit or by following the 15-percent-of-bill rule.

A tip should be deserved. The whole idea of tipping is for satisfactory service rendered. If the service is poor or the personnel rude, reduce the tip. If the service is very bad, leave no tip at all.

A tip may be left on the table (if in a restaurant), handed directly to the person performing the service, or put on a credit card as you sign for the bill.

Persons to tip	*Amount*
barber	$1 or more
bellhop (in hotel)	$1 per bag
carry-out person (at grocery store)	50¢ to $1 (total, depending on number of bags)
chambermaid (in hotel)	$3 to $10 (total, depending on length of stay)

checkroom attendant	25¢ if charge is 75¢; 50¢ for more than one coat
hairstylist (except owner of shop)	15% of bill
musician (for playing special request)	$1
parking attendant	50¢ to $1
shoeshine person	50¢ to $1
skycap (at airports)	50¢ to $1 per bag
taxi driver	50¢ for up to $1.50 fare; 15% of bill for higher fare
tour bus guide	50¢ to $1 per person
waiter or *waitress* (in restaurant, also for room service in hotel)	15% of bill
waiter, head (for special service—such as arrangements for room or for extra plates—for party of 10 or more)	$5 or more
washroom attendant	50¢ to $1

Appendix E
Situations to Ponder

Betsy

Betsy was a beautiful sixteen-year-old. Her two brothers had grown up and married. She had center stage at home, at least when her parents were there. Her mother was a nurse, working irregular hours, and her father, a pastor, was busy meeting the needs of the parishioners.

Betsy had always been dependable and was a favorite baby-sitter. She professed a faith in Christ, but her desire obviously was to walk with the world. Her parents were disturbed by her "worldly" interests, but they were confident that she was just going through a phase that would soon pass.

For about a year she had been seeing a "friend"—a mixed-up young man, a part-time drug user who needed a bit of counseling from a young woman who seemed to have it all together. Her parents would never have been in favor of a serious relationship, but that did not appear to be in the picture. However, one day Betsy tearfully made the announcement, "I'm pregnant."

The days that followed were tumultuous. Endless decisions, tears, heartache, anger, sleepless nights—how could this have happened?

Betsy had her baby. Her two remaining years of high school had to be put on hold. The already overstretched financial budget of her parents was stretched even further.

Betsy's life rapidly changed. It soon consisted of diapers, early morning feedings, colic, and seemingly endless tears. There would be no more sessions with her friends and the giant-size pizzas. Betsy's life had taken a very drastic turn.

The emotional adjustment for Betsy and her parents was almost insurmountable. All of her hopes and dreams had to be shifted, if not totally abandoned.

Jim

Jim Reeves came home from school one evening, dropped his books, spread a bit of peanut butter on some crackers, flipped on the TV, and stretched his lanky frame on the sofa, settling down to a Perry Mason mystery while waiting for dinner. This was the daily routine he had been following for a few weeks.

But today was different. His mother, who appeared to be busy in the kitchen, waited for the commercial and then, approaching the sofa, moved his long legs aside and sat beside him.

"Jim," she said, "for some reason I've been feeling very strongly that it is just not good for you to have a steady diet of Perry Mason each evening. When you were an infant, your dad and I, in the presence of witnesses, dedicated you to the Lord. We asked for wisdom and knowledge, and we vowed to bring you up in the nurture and admonition of the Lord. I feel now that I have to ask you to make this your last episode of Perry Mason, at least for a little while."

Without comment, Jim rose from the sofa, turned off the TV, picked up his books, and headed upstairs to his room.

"Oh, I didn't mean that you have to turn it off today, right in the middle of the program," she said.

"That's okay, Mom," he replied. "I've got a lot of homework I need to do anyway. Just call me when dinner is ready." A bit of understanding was all it took.

"Old Ivory"

A minister's wife tells of visiting a farm home in Maine, where she saw a very beautiful set of bone china in an old cupboard. The pattern, she was told, was "Old Ivory," a very popular pattern at the turn of the century. Now, many years later, it is rare and valuable.

She commented on the beauty of the china to the lady of the house, who said, "Oh, yes, I'm very proud of that set of china. It is one of the very few wedding gifts I have left. John had his very last meal on that china before he went to be with the Lord. I'm giving the set to my daughter-in-law. I want her to have it."

The following week the minister and his wife called on Jane, the daughter-in-law, in her home. Jane was busy arranging a vase of daffodils for the garden club meeting that afternoon.

The minister's wife noticed a single piece of "Old Ivory" on the table where Jane was working. She gazed at it a moment and said, "I'm admiring that beautiful piece of 'Old Ivory.'"

Jane turned and said, "That? I understand Jim's mother is giving me a whole set of it. I don't care for it. I just don't understand why she has to push it off on me. What does she expect me to do with it? Perhaps I can give it to a church benefit sometime."

It's easy to see that Jane was lacking in understanding. The china was only an expression of love for her, or perhaps it was a way for Jim's mother to say that she considered Jane "special" and deserving of something that meant much to her. Perhaps later Jane came to realize that a gift should be received in the same spirit in which it was given. Also, values change. She could not see today what might become valuable at a later day. And what about Jim? Jane surely was lacking in consideration for those around her.

Wally

Wally had difficulty keeping a job. Six months was about as long as he could last anywhere. He was a likable, good-hearted young man, not afraid of work. However, he had one fault. He enjoyed talking on the telephone, and he used company time to keep up his social contacts. Somehow Wally wasn't aware that he was actually stealing from his employer. He learned the hard way.

Brad

Brad and his parents redecorated his room. They painted it and put up new draperies, and although funds were in short supply, they stretched the budget to get a new bedspread. Brad felt like a king in a castle.

Some time later, his mother opened the door to his room to show off the family project to a neighbor. She wasn't sure she had opened the door to Brad's room! Things weren't the same. Why?

Brad had allowed his big German shepherd the run of his room. The dog had soiled the spread, chewed the chair legs, and given the room a definite dog odor. What a waste of time, effort, and expense! Brad's castle had become his doghouse and his mother's embarrassment.

Bibliography

Aresty, Esther B. *The Best Behavior*. New York: Simon & Schuster, 1970.

Baldrige, Letitia. *Letitia Baldrige's Complete Guide to a Great Social Life*. New York: Rawson Associates, 1987.

Beery, Mary. *Manners Made Easy*. New York: McGraw-Hill, 1954.

Carlson, Dale, and Don Fitzgibbon. *Manners That Matter*. New York: E. P. Dutton, 1983.

Frost, Marjorie. *Charming You*. Grand Rapids: Zondervan, 1968.

Harley, Frances Clay. *The Key to the Constitution of the United States*. Daytona Beach, Fla.: Patriotic Education, Inc., n.d.

Haupt, Enid A. *New Seventeen Book of Etiquette and Young Living*. New York: David McKay Co., Inc., 1963.

Maus, Cynthia Pearl. *Christ and the Fine Arts*. New York: Harper & Brothers, 1938.

Orr, William W. *Christians Should Have Good Manners Too*. Wheaton, Ill.: Scripture Press.

Post, Elizabeth L. *The Emily Post Book of Etiquette for Young People*. Emily Post Institute, Inc./New York: Funk & Wagnalls, 1967.

Post, Emily. *Etiquette*. New York: Harper & Row, 1984.

Smith, Whitney. *Flag Book of the United States*. New York: Morrow, 1970.

———. *Flags Through the Ages and Across the World*. New York: McGraw Hill, 1975.

Vanderbilt, Amy. *The Amy Vanderbilt Complete Book of Etiquette*. New York: Doubleday, 1978.

———. *Everyday Etiquette*. New York: Doubleday, 1978.

Word of Life Clubs CCF Bible Study Series. Schroon Lake, N.Y.: Word of Life Clubs, 1986.

Index